Walter B

D0468195

LUCENT LIBRARY *of* HISTORICAL ERAS

LIFE AND WORSHIP IN ANCIENT MESOPOTAMIA

LUCENT LIBRARY *of* HISTORICAL ERAS

LIFE AND WORSHIP IN ANCIENT MESOPOTAMIA

DON NARDO

LUCENT BOOKS
A part of Gale, Cengage Learning

GALE
CENGAGE Learning™

Detroit • New York • San Francisco • New Haven, Conn • Waterville, Maine • London

LIBRARY OF CONGRESS CATALOGING-IN-PUBLICATION DATA

Nardo, Don, 1947–
  Life and worship in ancient Mesopotamia / by Don Nardo.
    p. cm. — (Lucent library of historical eras)
  Includes bibliographical references and index.
  ISBN 978-1-4205-0100-1 (hardcover)
  1. Iraq—Civilization—To 634—Juvenile literature. 2. Iraq—Social life and customs—Juvenile literature. 3. Iraq—Religion—Juvenile literature.
  I. Title.
  DS69.5.N32 2008
  935—dc22
                                                        2008022047

Lucent Books
27500 Drake Rd.
Farmington Hills, MI 48331

ISBN-13: 978-1-4205-0100-1
ISBN-10: 1-4205-0100-3

J935
Nardo
27 June 09

Printed in the United States of America
1 2 3 4 5 6 7 12 11 10 09 08

Contents

Foreword

Looking back from the vantage point of the present, history can be viewed as a myriad of intertwining roads paved by human events. Some paths stand out—broad highways whose mileposts, even from a distance of centuries, are clear. The events that propelled the rise to power of Germany's Third Reich, its role in World War II, and its eventual demise, for example, are well defined and documented.

Other roads are less distinct, their route sometimes hidden from view. Modern legislatures may have developed from old tribal councils, for example, but the links between them are indistinct in places, open to discussion and interpretation.

The architecture of civilization—law, religion, art, science, and government—as well as the more everyday aspects of our culture—what we eat, what we wear—all developed along the historical roads and byways. In that progression can be traced every facet of modern life.

A broad look back along these roads reveals that many paths—though of vastly different character—seem to converge at a few critical junctions. These intersections are those great historical eras that echo over the long, steady course of human history, extending beyond the past and into the present.

These epic periods of time are the focus of Historical Eras. They shine through the mists of history like beacons, illuminated by a burst of creativity that propels events forward—so bright that we, from thousands of years away, can clearly see the chain of events leading to the present.

Each Historical Eras consists of a set of books that highlight various aspects of these major eras. For example, the Elizabethan England library features volumes on Queen Elizabeth I and her court, Elizabethan theater, the great playwrights, and everyday life in Elizabethan London.

The mini-library approach allows for the division of each era into its most significant and most interesting parts and the exploration of those parts in depth. Also, social and cultural trends as well as illustrative documents and eyewitness accounts can be prominently featured in individual volumes.

Historical Eras presents a wealth of information to young readers. The lively narrative, fully documented primary and secondary source quotations, maps, photographs, sidebars, and annotated bibliographies serve as launching points for class discussion and further research.

In studying the great historical eras, students also develop a better understanding of our own times. What we learn from the past and how we apply it in the present may shape the future and may determine whether our era will be a guiding light to those traveling future roads.

◆ Introduction

THE PAST IS PRESENT

Almost everyone is familiar with the adages "there is nothing new under the sun," "the past is present," and "the more things change, the more they stay the same." These common old sayings have particular relevance for the Middle East. When talking about this pivotal and turbulent region as it was before the modern era, scholars use the term *Near East*. Lying more or less in the center of the ancient Near East was Mesopotamia, a wide expanse of windswept plains dominated by the Tigris and Euphrates rivers. Those meandering waterways still flow through the area, which became part of the country of Iraq when it was established in the 1930s.

Archaeologists who excavated Mesopotamian cities in Iraq in the nineteenth and twentieth centuries discovered more than old temples, palaces, statues, pottery jars, and clay tablets bearing ancient pictures and writing. They also found that many aspects of the everyday lives of the region's ancient inhabitants were the same, or almost the same, as those of modern Iraqis. In many ways, indeed, the customs and habits of today's Middle East mirror those of the ancient Near East.

Urban Markets and Houses

One of the more striking examples of such continuity between the area's ancient and modern cultures is the highly recognizable, ever-present street market. The renowned twentieth-century British archaeologist Charles Leonard Woolley, who excavated the ancient Sumerian urban center, or city, of Ur, said that its market was much like those in Iraqi towns and cities today. In the words of another great pioneer of Near Eastern archaeology, Samuel N. Kramer, both

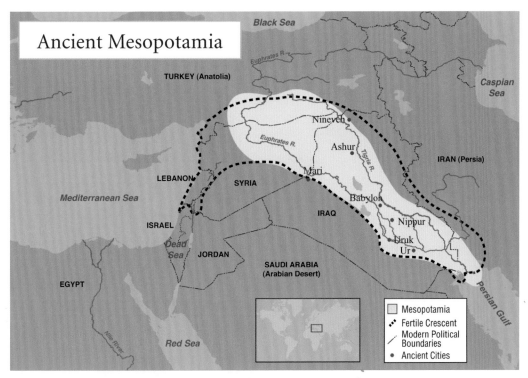

Ancient Mesopotamia

Mesopotamia is situated in the center of the ancient Near East.

the ancient and modern urban markets feature

a maze of narrow passages shielded from the blazing sun by awnings and lined with booths. Here the city dweller could choose his daily groceries from a wide range of foodstuffs that included onions, beans, and cucumbers; dates and apples and other fruits; cheese and spices; dried fish, mutton, pork, [and] duck. Here, too, he could find displayed alongside the pots, clothing, and other local products . . . imported luxuries [such as] beads from Iran.[1]

As remains true in Iraqi and other Middle Eastern towns, ancient Mesopotamian markets were surrounded by houses made of mud bricks. Both the ancient and modern versions typically have inner courtyards at least partly open to the sky. This allows the residents to take advantage of the region's abundant sunlight. (It experiences at least three hundred sunny days each year.) Courtyards also provide welcome ventilation on summer days, when temperatures can soar to 120°F (49°C) or more. "Naturally," noted scholar Gwendolyn Leick points out, the ancient Mesopotamians "had no telegraph poles, asphalted roads, [or] satellite dishes." And they lacked the "electricity to light up

An Iraqi man prays near a satellite dish in the courtyard of his mud-brick home in Baghdad. Modern amenities aside, homes in the region today share the same basic architectural features as those in ancient Mesopotamia.

shops and houses at night," which most modern Iraqis have. Yet "archaeologists have been struck by the fact that many architectural features of simple residential buildings have persisted over the last four thousand years."[2]

Timeless World of the Marshes

Another kind of house that has long been common in the region can be seen in the extensive marshes that stretch across parts of southeastern Iraq. (The modern Iraqi dictator Saddam Hussein drained most of the marshes, which had existed for thousands of years, so that his enemies could not hide in them; but after his fall in 2003, the Iraqi government began restoring the marshes.) Many of the marsh dwellers build houses from the reeds that grow in these waterways, just as their Mesopotamian ancestors did. A surviving Sumerian stone carving dating from the third millennium (the 2000s) B.C., shows a reed house with an arched roof identical to that in modern versions.

Up until the last few years of the twentieth century, the Iraqi marsh dwellers also fashioned canoes of reeds, as their ancient counterparts did. And they still used long poles tipped with metal prongs to catch fish swimming through that watery, timeless world. In addition, the male inhabitants of Iraq's marshes played a game in which they stood up in their canoes and tried to knock one another into the water; the ancient marsh dwellers played the same game.

An Iraqi named Salim Kerkush, born in 1949, remembers these and other honored traditions of the marshes. He says that his father and grandfather lived very much as the ancient Sumerian and Babylonian marsh dwellers did. "It was a very simple life," he states, recalling his childhood. "We would fish. We would collect

An Iraqi man stands outside a house made of reeds that ancient stone carvings show is like those built by Mesopotamian marsh-dwellers thousands of years ago.

the reeds. We would plant rice." In the marshes, he adds, one often encountered "stars reflected in dark water, the croakings of frogs, canoes coming home at evening, peace and continuity, the stillness of a world that never knew an engine."[3]

Religion and War

Another similarity between ancient Mesopotamia and modern Iraq is the religious devotion of the residents. The Sumerians, Babylonians, Assyrians, Persians, and other ancient peoples who lived in the region were extremely

Men navigate their canoes through the marshes of modern-day Iraq much as their ancestors did in ancient Mesopotamia.

religious and spiritual. They worshiped a large pantheon (group) of gods. And they believed that these deities heard human prayers and sometimes intervened in people's lives or the affairs of nations. To show their devotion, the Mesopotamians erected temples and other religious structures in their cities. Today's Iraqis are mostly Muslims whose faith, Islam, recognizes only one god. Yet they are no less devout than their long-dead ancestors, and like them, they build religious structures (called mosques) and strongly believe in the power of prayer.

In recent decades many Iraqis have relied on their religious beliefs to help them cope with the constant wars that have ravaged the region. Sometimes they have fought among themselves. But more often, outside powers have invaded. A similar pattern prevailed in ancient times, when Mesopotamia was frequently the site of battles, military campaigns, and wars of conquest.

Thus in many ways the past truly is the present in a region that long ago witnessed the rise of the first cities, the invention of writing, and the almost constant clash of competing empires. As University of Windsor scholar Stephen Bertman aptly puts it:

In the main, yesterday's Mesopotamia is today's Iraq, a war-torn land where people still struggle to eke out their daily lives as did their ancestors thousands of years ago. Yet buried in Iraq's barren desert there also lie the ruins of an earlier glory and splendor that once shone for all to see.[4]

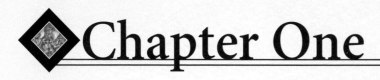

Chapter One

HOUSES AND THEIR CONTENTS

Everyday life in ancient Mesopotamia was generally divided into two broad and mostly separate spheres (areas or domains). These were life in the cities, or urban life, and life in the countryside, or rural life. Surviving evidence for rural life in the region is scanty at best. This is because the small huts in which rural farmers and villagers dwelled were made of highly perishable materials such as branches, reeds, and hard-packed mud. Most traces of them have long since disappeared.

Much more is known about urban life, partly because small parts of a number of townhouses and the artifacts within them have survived. Also, the numerous significant societal innovations and fruits of civilization created in ancient Mesopotamia (including the invention of writing) came almost entirely from the cities. After the Sumerians erected the world's first cities there in the late 4000s B.C., it

remained primarily an urban society for the rest of ancient times.

These thriving urban centers—among them Ur, Nippur, Lagash, Ashur, Mari, Nineveh, and the famous Babylon—also featured two separate living spheres: life in the home and life in the community. When involved in community activities outside the home, people had to meet and converse with all manner of non–family members, some of them strangers. And they had to adapt to the brisk pace of life that has characterized urban settings everywhere ever since.

In contrast, the home provided a private sanctuary, a small and confined but familiar and comfortable little world. There, surrounded by relatives, a person could feel safe from the hustle and bustle, uncertainties, and dangers that lurked outside. At home, the chief activities and concerns were raising children, preparing and cooking food, cleaning and conducting home repairs, dressing, and doing personal grooming.

Houses: Materials and Layout

Almost all of the houses in Sumerian and other ancient Mesopotamian cities were made of mud, or clay, bricks that had been dried in the sun. Whenever possible, the outer—along with some of the inner—walls were several feet thick to help protect the interiors from the heat of the day. (Also, people usually whitewashed the exterior walls to reflect away some of the incoming sunlight.) Another reason the brick walls of houses were often thick was to ensure the stability and durability of these structures. Thinner walls were more likely to erode, crack, and collapse than thicker ones; also, it

The ruins of the palace of King Nebuchadnezzar revealed that the structure had a bathroom with a shower chamber lined with waterproofed bricks, a luxury only found in the homes of a few royals and nobles.

Reliable but Impermanent Mud Bricks

Almost all houses in ancient Mesopotamia were built of mud bricks, which were made of either clay or a mixture of clay and various binding materials, such as straw or sand. Most often workers pressed the resulting "mud" into wooden or pottery molds and then left them out in the sun to dry. Obviously the summer, when the sun was at its hottest, was the most opportune time to make bricks. And appropriately the first month of summer came to be called the "month of bricks." People also sometimes fired the bricks in kilns, which made them harder and long lasting. But the scarcity of wood in the region to fuel the kilns made fired bricks more expensive. So they were used mainly for high-status buildings such as palaces. Workers often used some kind of mortar between the bricks, such as a plaster made by mixing moist mud with powdered lime. Bitumen, a tarlike substance found in scattered ground-level deposits, was also used for mortar. It had the added benefit of being more or less waterproof. Unfortunately no matter what kind of mortar was used, mud bricks rapidly deteriorated, creating the need for frequent repairs.

was easier for thieves to tunnel through thinner walls.

In some times and places in the region, the builders' legal responsibility may also have determined the thickness and sturdiness of house walls. In Babylonia in the early to mid-second millennium B.C., for instance, builders who did sloppy work may have been subject to penalties. These were laid out in the famous law code of King Hammurabi (reigned ca. 1792–1750 B.C.). One of his laws stated: "If a builder builds a house for someone, even though he has not yet completed it, [and] if then the walls seem [to be] toppling, the builder must make the walls solid from his own means [i.e., at his own expense]." The punishments were much more harsh if someone was hurt as a result of the builder's carelessness:

> If a builder builds a house for someone, and does not construct it properly, and the house which he built falls in and kills its owner, then that builder shall be put to death. . . . If it kills the son of the [house's] owner, the son of that builder shall be put to death.[5]

These mud-brick townhouses varied in size and quality according to their owners' wealth. Those of poorer folk measured roughly 8 feet by 18 feet (2.4m by 5.4m) and had two to four small rooms. Considerably larger were houses belonging to government administrators, well-to-do merchants, and other successful individuals. Such dwellings featured several rooms arranged on two floors, with one or two sturdy brick staircases leading to the upper story. Typical were the upscale Sumerian townhouses in Nippur, several of which were excavated by teams from Chicago's Oriental Institute in the second half of the twentieth century. The plans of these dwellings, Leick writes,

> reflect the pattern still common in the Middle East nowadays: a single doorway leads into a large courtyard surrounded by various rooms and storage facilities. Private rooms are arranged behind or at either side of a reception room. In larger houses it was possible to separate public and private spaces by one or more additional courtyards.[6]

In such two-story houses, the kitchen was on the ground floor and often opened into the courtyard. A brick hearth situated along one kitchen wall provided cooking facilities.

A majority of homes had no bathrooms in the modern sense. The average person relieved him- or herself into an earthen pot and periodically emptied it into a communal pit dug for that purpose on the edge of town. Most people bathed in the nearest river or canal. Or they lugged buckets of water into the house to moisten cloths for what today would be called a "sponge bath." (Water from both buckets and cisterns, shallow basins that caught rainwater, was also used for cooking and drinking.)

Owners of a few larger houses could afford to install small bathrooms featuring latrine-like toilets. The waste was dropped into buckets or drained through baked-clay channels to cesspools located just outside the house. Only the royal palaces and perhaps a few mansions belonging to rich nobles had bathrooms in which one could take a shower (although a crude one by modern standards). The palace of the Babylonian king Nebuchadnezzar II (ca. 605–562 B.C.), for example, had such a luxury. The room's lower walls and floor were lined with fired bricks coated with a tarlike substance to waterproof them. The king sat or stood in the center of the chamber while servants gently poured containers of water over him. The dirty water drained into clay or stone channels in the floor that carried it outside.

Household Furnishings

The amount and quality of the furnishings of these ancient townhouses also varied according to the owners' financial means. Common furniture items in poorer homes included stools and chairs made of palm wood (the cheapest, softest variety of wood in the region) and/or woven reeds. There might have been one or two low wooden tables, too, for eating daily meals or stacking personal belongings. Reed baskets or containers made of baked clay or palm wood were also employed for storage, because closets had not yet been invented. Most people slept on beds consisting of reed mats or crude mattresses stuffed with palm fibers (which must have been lumpy).

By comparison, well-off and noble families enjoyed the comfort of sleeping on beds with wooden frames and softer mattresses stuffed with wool or goat's hair. These folks could also afford the luxury of linen sheets and woolen blankets. In addition, larger homes had plenty of wooden chairs, some upholstered, like modern ones, with leather or felt. Yale

A carbonized wooden arm rest of a chair from the mid-third millennium B.C. contains decorative carvings and shell pieces.

A Mesopotamian Recipe

This ancient Babylonian recipe, dating from around 1700 B.C. (3,700 years ago), is for "tarru-bird stew." (Tarru birds may have been pigeons, quail, or partridges.)

[I]n addition to the tarru] meat from a fresh leg of mutton is needed. Boil the water, throw fat in. Dress the tarru [and place in pot]. Add coarse salt as needed.

[Add] hulled cake of malt. Squeeze onions, leek, garlic [together] and add to pot along [with] milk. After [cooking and] cutting up the tarru, plunge them [to braise] in stock [from the pot]. Then place them back in the pot [in order to finish cooking]. To be brought out for carving.

Quoted in "Mesopotamian Menus." www.saudiaramco world.com/issue/198802/mesopotamian.menus.htm.

University scholar Karen Nemet-Nejat, an expert on ancient Mesopotamian life, describes the wide variety of chairs that surviving evidence shows existed in finer Mesopotamian households:

Chairs had legs, backs, and even arms. Their frames were made from various hardwoods; seventeen kinds of wood were listed [in texts found in the ruins of Mari, on the upper Euphrates]. Sometimes chair frames were inlaid with copper, bronze, silver, gold or carved ivory. Chairs were often painted. . . . Loose linen slipcovers were even designed for [them].[7]

More evidence shows that some wealthy Assyrians lounged on sofas upholstered and decorated similarly to the finer chairs. They ate their meals at tables constructed of hardwoods imported from Syria and Palestine. And they used linen tablecloths and napkins, along with plates, bowls, cups, and trays of finely fashioned wood, pottery, or metals.

Common Foods and Dishes

Well-off Mesopotamians could afford other mealtime luxuries as well. On the one hand, they had full-time cooks and other kitchen workers, who prepared varied, highly appetizing dishes. On the other, they ate meat on a regular basis, perhaps every day. In contrast, people of average or poorer means ate mostly dishes made from cereals (grains), supplemented by a few vegetables and fruits and sometimes fish. (Poor people only rarely ate meat, usually during major religious festivals.)

A few foods and dishes were common to both poor and wealthy households, notably bread and porridge. Among the grains used to make these staples were barley, emmer wheat, and rye. A flat, unleavened bread made from coarse flour was widely consumed, but breads made from more finely ground, more expensive flour were available only for those who could afford them. People often mixed milk, sesame seed oil, fish oil, or even fruit juices or grated cheese into the dough, giving it a heartier consistency.

Among the available vegetables, the most popular were onions and garlic, used by both poor and rich people in a wide variety of dishes. Other common vegetables included peas, cabbage, lentils, carrots, radishes, and beets. Fruits eaten across the region included apricots, dates, apples, cherries, figs, and plums. Because the Mesopotamians did not raise bees (as the Egyptians did), they lacked honey (except when imported, which was expensive); so the most common food sweetener was date juice, extracted from the date palm.

The main meat products, for the families who could afford them, were pork, mutton (from sheep), deer, gazelle, and birds including ducks and geese. Most of these were used immediately after slaughter, since the weather in the Tigris-Euphrates valley is often hot, and refrigeration did not yet exist. (So the meat tended to spoil quickly.) However, some meat was preserved for a while by salting, drying in the sun, or smoking. For poorer families that could not afford meat, fishing was a cheap alternative. The region supported more than fifty kinds of fish, which also supplied the main ingredient of a tasty sauce widely used as a spice.

Some of the ways in which ancient Mesopotamian cooks prepared meat dishes and other fare are known thanks to the discovery of part of a cookbook (written on clay tablets). Dating from about 1700 B.C., it seems to be the work of the chef of the king of Mari. The text on the tablets consists of thirty-five recipes, including those for "bird stew," "gazelle broth," and "Assyrian stew." It is important to note that this cookbook was not intended to be used by ordinary Mesopotamian folk in their home kitchens, as one modern observer explains:

> Concise, these recipes are not for the culinary amateur. Often just a few lines long, they summarize essential steps and ingredients . . . ignoring quantities and cooking times, which their users were apparently expected to know from experience. A far cry from the cookbooks of today, they were not meant to guide the housewife . . . but mainly to standardize and even ritualize cooking procedures. In 1700 BC, after all, writing, and therefore also reading, was a professional rather than a general skill.[8]

Clothing Styles and Grooming

Archaeological evidence also gives some idea of what the residents of ancient Mesopotamian homes wore. In the fourth

Beer and Wine

The most popular beverage among most ancient Mesopotamians was beer, which they made primarily from barley. Beer was so popular, in fact, that

there was a goddess of beer brewing, named Ninkasi. Local brewers produced more than seventy varieties of beer, which varied in potency, clarity, sweetness, and so on. Wine was another popular drink. But it was more expensive, in part because grapes grew well mainly in the hill country of northern Assyria. So the majority of wines consumed in Mesopotamia had to be imported from Syria or Palestine, and for the most part only well-to-do people could afford them.

Cuneiform notations on a clay tablet from the third century B.C. list monthly barley rations for a group of gardeners. Ancient Mesopotamians used barley to brew beer.

millennium B.C., and earlier, it appears that men and women mostly donned sheepskins or goatskins. Men went shirtless and wore their skins ankle length. In contrast, women made sure the skins covered them above the waist, except for one shoulder, purposely left bare.

Textiles, another important Mesopotamian contribution to human civilization, replaced animal skins in the third millen-

nium B.C. The most commonly used fabric was sheep's wool. Charles Leonard Woolley's excavations at Ur uncovered small fragments of bright red wool cloth, which he believed were from garments worn by women who marched in a funeral procession for a deceased king, queen, or other royal person. He later speculated: "It must have been a very gaily dressed crowd that assembled in the open mat-lined pit for

An illustration shows the variety of men's clothing styles worn by the Babylonians and Assyrians in ancient Mesopotamia. Details include robes and tunics of varying lengths, colored fabrics, hats, and footwear.

the royal [funeral ceremonies], a blaze of color with the crimson [red] coats, [with] the silver [trim], and the gold [trim]."⁹ While wool was widely used to cover the body, felt (made from crushed sheep's hair) was a common material for accessories such as shoes and hats. No cotton was used in the region until the Assyrians started importing it from Egypt in about 700 B.C. Later still, in the early first millennium A.D., silk began to be imported from faraway China.

At the start of the Akkadian Empire (about 2300 B.C.), fashions in the region underwent noticeable change. Many men began wearing long robes that draped over one shoulder, whereas women now covered both shoulders and allowed their necklines to plunge into an open V-neck. These styles remained widely popular for several centuries.

Then, in about 1400 B.C., another major clothing change swept through the Mesopotamian cities. As Nemet-Nejat explains, the evidence for this transformation takes two forms:

> The main source comes from art objects, such as sculptures, bas-reliefs, plaques, carved ivories, and cylinder seals [small carved objects used to stamp impressions into moist clay]. [Written] texts also catalogued many words related to clothing, [including] different qualities of textiles, from cheap materials for servants to those worn by royalty.[10]

This evidence shows that Assyrian men and women began wearing wide robes belted at the waist, with tassels hanging down between the legs. Decorated kilts also became a popular form of male attire. Somewhat later, many men in Assyria and other parts of Mesopotamia chose to wear short-sleeved, belted tunics that stretched from the neck to the knees. This basic garment remained fairly standard for average residents of the region for a long time to come. People, especially members of the upper classes, frequently accessorized these outfits. For example, they added outer cloaks, jewelry, trousers (popular among Persian men), caps, and/or walking sticks.

Upper-class individuals also engaged in elaborate, often expensive grooming activities, including using cosmetics. (The extent to which people in the lower, working classes did so is unknown.)

Items found among the ruins of a royal tomb show how women from the upper classes in ancient Mesopotamia accessorized their outfits with jewelry and hair ornaments.

Parts of women's makeup kits were found in the royal cemetery at Ur, including small pieces of blue, green, yellow, red, and black eye makeup (made from antimony, a metal-like substance found in some mineral ores). One applied it with a wooden or ivory pin.

Women were not the only ones who used makeup. In his biography of the great Persian king Cyrus II (559–530 B.C.), the fourth-century B.C. Greek historian Xenophon wrote: "He encouraged also the fashion of [men] penciling the eyes, that they might seem more lustrous than they are, and of using cosmetics to make the complexion look better than nature made it."[11]

Other common grooming items used in ancient Mesopotamia included wooden and ivory combs, metal tweezers, and hand mirrors made of highly polished copper, bronze, and silver. The discovery of such familiar objects, which remain in wide use today, provides yet another vital link between ourselves and those who created the first civilizations.

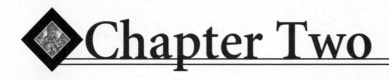

Chapter Two

FAMILY, WOMEN, AND CHILDREN

Each of the many houses in Ur, Nippur, Ashur, Babylon, Mari, and other Mesopotamian cities was the home of a family, society's most basic unit.

Because the surviving evidence is somewhat vague, modern scholars are uncertain about the size and structure of the average family. In fact there may have been no typical family across the region and throughout antiquity (ancient times). Depending on the place and era, some families may have been nuclear—consisting of a father, a mother, and their children. Others may have been extended—with aunts, cousins, grandparents, and/or in-laws cohabiting with the nuclear group in the same house. Some evidence suggests that a mix of nuclear and extended families existed in the Sumerian cities in the third millennium B.C., and that most families in Assyria and Babylonia in the millennium that followed were small and nuclear.

More certain is that the vast majority of ancient Mesopotamian families were patriarchal, or male dominated. They were also patrileneal. That is, the father (*abum* in Akkadian, the language spoken by the Assyrians and Babylonians) was the head of the household. And the house and other family property passed from a father to his son (*marum*) or sons when the father died. When the inherited property was divided among two or more individuals, both law and custom attempted to make the process orderly and fair. "Various measures could be taken to limit the negative effects" of divided inheritances, Leick writes. The male heirs "could assign contiguous [adjoining] fields to one brother or opt for co-residence and the pooling of their portions. Another possibility was for one brother to buy out his siblings. Not only

A relief shows King Ur-Nanshe of Lagash, carrying a basket on his head, and his wife and children. Although little is known about the size and structure of the average family in ancient Mesopotamia, it was most certainly a patriarchal society.

could fields and houses be inherited, but also slaves and temple offices."[12]

As for the mother (*ummum*), she remained under her husband's control throughout the marriage. Most marriages were monogamous (having one man and one woman), although kings and other very wealthy men sometimes took extra wives and/or concubines (live-in mistresses). Any daughter (*martum*) born in the family was also expected to be obedient to the father until she got married; then she passed into her husband's charge.

High-Status Women

Just as detailed evidence about family structure is lacking, only scattered facts about the status and lives of ancient Mesopotamian women have survived. Even the records for royal women are scant, as scholar Steven J. Garfinkle points out in reference to the ancient Assyrians:

The surviving records overwhelmingly document the activities of the king and his elite at court. [Moreover] this is largely the history of a male elite. There are rare exceptions . . . but for the most part the women of the Assyrian court are not prominently attested in the historical record.[13]

Priestesses like the one depicted in this statue found at the Temple of Ishtar in Mari were held in high esteem in ancient Mesopotamian society.

Of the exceptions—those royal women who *have* survived in the records—queens and princesses in the Sumerian city of Ur seem to have enjoyed unusually high status. Part of the evidence for this was uncovered in the city's royal cemetery, excavated by Woolley and others. The graves of queens (some of whom may also have served as high priestesses) are just as rich and elaborate as those of their husbands and sons. "It appears," Leick writes, that, "at least at Ur, it was possible for some female[s] to achieve considerable political and religious influence."[14]

Whatever the status of queens in ancient Sumer and Babylonia, priestesses seem to have commanded respect and high social status. Among them were those who officiated in temples of Inanna (or Ishtar), goddess of love and war. Also, at Sippar and other cities in the early second millennium B.C., some temples featured female personnel, possibly priestesses, known as *naditu*. Some evidence indicates that they performed daily sacrifices and prayers. Apparently they lived secluded lives in a nunnery-like building called a *gagum* ("locked house") and had to remain both celibate and childless (although there were exceptions in certain cities). These women must have been held in high esteem because they were allowed to own estates and other property and manage them as men did.

Status and Duties of Ordinary Women

It would be misleading, however, to judge all ancient Mesopotamian women by the evidence from a handful of queens and priestesses. These privileged women were definitely not the norm. As one expert puts it, they "were regarded as set apart from the customary female roles."[15]

One important observation can be made about Mesopotamian women in general: They lacked political rights, so they could not hold public office or rule a city or nation (with the rare exception of a few queens who ruled temporarily after their husbands died). Some evidence suggests that women's legal status was somewhat higher in the Sumerian cities in the third millennium B.C., than it was in Assyrian and Babylonian society later. Also, it is possible that women in poor farm households shared equally in the decision making with their husbands (a situation common in many parts of ancient Europe). But overall, Mesopotamian women throughout antiquity were second-class citizens who did the bidding of their fathers and husbands.

In spite of their general subservience to men, most ancient Mesopotamian women were allowed to work, which allowed them a degree of freedom that was rare in many other ancient regions, including Greece. Some Babylonian women even held jobs usually performed by men. There were some female scribes in the early second millennium B.C., for instance, at least ten of them at Mari alone. Surviving sources from that period also mention a few women doctors and artists.

Respect and Happiness in Old Age

Some ancient Mesopotamian queens were highly respected and influential in the royal court. The mother of the Neo-Babylonian king Nabonidus (reigned ca. 555–539 B.C.), Addu-Guppi, was one of them. After her death, the king honored her memory with an inscription (in the first person, as if she had written it). It reads in part:

[T]he gods] gave me, a woman, an exalted position and a famous name in the country. [I have spent] one hundred and four happy years in that piety which Sin [or Nanna, the moon god] has planted in my heart. My eyesight was good to the end of my life, my hearing excellent, my hands and feet were sound, my words were well-chosen, [and] my health was fine and my mind happy. I saw my great-great grandchildren . . . in good health and thus had my fill of old age.

Quoted in James B. Pritchard, *The Ancient Near East, Vol. 2.* Princeton: Princeton University Press, 1976, pp. 560–561.

Meanwhile, larger numbers of lower-class women labored on the land, helping their husbands plant, harvest, prune vines, and tow barges upriver. Other women worked in shops and factories, particularly those that produced textiles. (In ancient societies, a factory consisted of one or more large workrooms in which several people made products by hand.) It was also common for women to work as maids, cooks, and gardeners in palaces or on temple estates. In addition, some women were barmaids; and a few actually ran taverns. Still other women sang, danced, or played musical instruments to entertain the men who visited these establishments. Whatever their jobs, working women had to put up with blatant discrimination. They were paid only half of what men made for the same work. And women received no pay at all while they were menstruating (when society judged them to be unproductive).

The numbers or percentages of Mesopotamian women who held down jobs are unknown. It is likely that a majority of women stayed home. Like housewives in all ages and places, they gave birth, raised the children, cleaned, cooked, managed the household, and saw to their husbands' needs. Still, the situation of such women was not necessarily grim, because they did have a few economic rights granted by law or custom. For example, a daughter could inherit slaves or land if she had no brothers and her father approved. Women could also sue in court to obtain land or other property due them (although they could not be witnesses in court cases).

Marriage and Divorce

All of these factors—bearing children, maintaining the household, adhering to inheritance customs, and so forth—were part of the larger institution of marriage. Romantic love may have occasionally been involved. For the most part, however, marriage was viewed primarily as a means of producing children and thereby continuing society and its traditions. A majority of marital unions were arranged by relatives (usually fathers or grandfathers). Most brides were in their teens, while the grooms were typically in their twenties or thirties.

Because marriage was seen largely as a business arrangement, legal contracts had to be drawn up to make it binding. In Babylonia the union was equally invalid if it was not consummated by sex. One of the laws set down by King Hammurabi stated: "If a man take a woman to wife, but have no intercourse with her, this woman is no wife to him." As the wedding date approached, the groom (or his father or uncle) negotiated with the bride's father (or other guardian) about money matters. First and foremost, the bride's father promised to supply a dowry. This consisted of valuable items for her upkeep in the marriage, such as jewelry, dinnerware and cooking utensils, furniture, slaves, and/or bars of silver or other metals. If a Babylonian wife died,

A relief from the palace of King Ashurbanipal in Ninevah depicts a family with two children. Laws and traditions in ancient Mesopotamia addressed many details of marriage and divorce, including payment of dowries and issues of infertility and infidelity.

Fair Inheritance Laws

Among the more numerous and thorough family-related laws in Hammurabi's famous code are those dealing with inheritance. On the one hand, they go to considerable pains to honor the feelings and wishes of the deceased. In the following example, the legacy of the father's favorite son is protected:

If a man give to one of his sons, whom he prefers [over the others], a field, garden, and house, [and] if later the father die, and the brothers divide the estate, then they shall first give him [the favorite son] the present of his father, and he shall accept it; and the rest of the paternal property shall they divide.

Babylonian laws were also surprisingly fair-minded regarding the inheritance of property by women. The first part of one law reads: "If a father give a present to his daughter [and] then die, then she is to receive a portion as a child from the paternal estate, and enjoy [it] so long as she lives."

However, these laws were not so enlightened as to give women economic or legal rights equal to those of men. The second part of the law states: "Her estate belongs to her brothers," indicating that, though she could use her portion, it technically belonged to them.

Quoted in "The Code of Hammurabi," www.wsu.edu/~dee/MESO/CODE.HTM.

the dowry legally became the property of the children produced in the marriage. Another of Hammurabi's laws states: "If a man marry a woman, and she bear sons to him; if then this woman die, then shall her father have no claim on her dowry; this belongs to her sons."[16]

Another financial aspect of marriages was the "bride-price"—money and/or valuables that the groom's father might give the bride's family. This, like the dowry, could be paid in installments until the first child was born (when the balance had to be paid). Once these and other details of the marriage contract

were agreed to, the groom's father held a feast for the two families, at which time the marriage was seen to officially begin.

For those marriages that did not work out, divorce was sometimes an option. Among the legal grounds for divorce was wife beating or some other form of abuse by the husband, although the woman had to present proof of the mistreatment. If she could do so, she emerged in good shape. According to one of the Babylonian laws:

If a woman quarrel with her husband, and say: "You are not congenial to me [i.e., mistreat me]," the reasons for her prejudice must be presented. [If] there is no fault on her part, but he leaves and neglects her, then no guilt attaches to this woman. She shall take her dowry and go back to her father's house.[17]

Another common reason for divorce was the wife's infertility. If a Babylonian woman could not have children, her husband could leave her. But she was allowed to keep any moneys that were negotiated in the marriage contract, as stipulated in another of Hammurabi's laws: "If a man wishes to separate from his wife who has borne him no children, he shall give her the amount of her . . . dowry which she brought from her father's house, and let her go."[18]

The marriage might also end in divorce if one or the other partner was unfaithful. Also, if the wife was the cheater, she and her lover could, in theory, suffer a harsh punishment. Another Babylonian law said: "If a man's wife be surprised [in bed] with another man, both shall be tied and thrown into the water."[19] It is unlikely, however, that such extreme penalties were given out for adultery in most cases, since it was easier and more humane to simply get a divorce.

Having Children

In marriages that ended in divorce, any children involved might end up with either the father or the mother, depending on the situation. That children were

A Neo-Sumerian relief shows a woman nursing her child. The primitive state of medicine in ancient Mesopotamia resulted in many dangerous pregnancies and deliveries as well as a high infant mortality rate.

viewed as extremely important in most Mesopotamian cultures is illustrated by the fact that numerous laws pertained to their legal rights. The inheritance rights of sons were especially prominent in Hammurabi's law code, for instance. Not surprisingly, then, it was happy news for a family when a woman found that she was going to have a baby.

Yet pregnant mothers and their husbands and other relatives experienced a certain amount of fear and anxiety before the baby was born. These worries came partly from the primitive state of medicine at the time, which ensured a high infant death rate. (That rate may have been 30 percent or more, compared to less than 1 percent in the United States today.) The peculiar social and religious customs of the day were another factor. According to one scholar, typical haunting questions included "Will the child be born dead? Will it live only to become the one out of two that finally die? Will it be born deformed and need to be drowned in the river to avert evil?"[20] One way to ward off any evil that might affect the child was to wear amulets and other charms thought to have magical powers. One popular amulet depicted the male demon Pazu-

zu, who supposedly scared off the female demon Lamashtu, credited with causing miscarriages and crib death.

Almost all children were born in the home. During the delivery, female relatives and/or an experienced midwife attended to the mother. By the first millennium B.C., the use of birthing stools was common. In earlier eras, most mothers probably assumed a squatting stance (supported by her helpers) during the last stages of labor. People thought that if the mother wore a charm necklace made of twenty-one stones, the birth process would go easier. It was also customary for one of the helpers to rub the mother's abdomen with oil.

The new child received a name soon after birth. It nursed for two or more

Lullaby for a Little Prince

Among the surviving lullabies from ancient Mesopotamia is this one, recited to the son of the Sumerian king Shugli (reigned ca. 2094–2047 B.C.).

Ah, ah, may he grow sturdy through my crooning, may he flourish through my crooning! May he put down strong foundations as roots, may he spread branches wide like a *cakir* plant! Lord, from this you know our whereabouts; among those resplendent [impressive] apple trees overhanging

the river, may someone who passes by reach out his hand, may someone lying there raise his hand. My son, sleep will overtake you, sleep will settle on you. Sleep come, sleep come, sleep come to my son, sleep hasten to my son! Put to sleep his open eyes, settle your hand upon his sparkling eyes. As for his murmuring tongue, let the murmuring not spoil his sleep.

"Lullaby for a Son of Shugli," Electronic Text Corpus of Sumerian Literature. www-etcsl.orient.ox.ac.uk/ section2/tr24214.htm.

years. But if the mother could not produce milk and the family could not afford to hire a wet nurse, the child usually died. The baby spent most of its time in a basket lined with linen.

Little evidence has survived for the manner in which ancient Mesopotamian peoples raised their children as they grew. Youngsters did play with toys, as shown by several toys found by archaeologists. Among these are baby rattles made of baked clay; dolls and miniature furniture for young girls; slingshots, bows, and miniature chariots for young boys; and balls, hoops, and jump ropes for both genders. In rural areas, children were also expected to help with farm work, although the age at which this began is uncertain.

If a husband and wife could not have children of their own, they often adopted one or more. Their main motivation was to make sure there was someone to care for them in their old age. The simplest form of adoption was rescuing a baby who had been abandoned. Older children were adopted, too, usually by signing a contract with someone who agreed to give up a child. A surviving adoption contract from Mari in the eighteenth century B.C. shows that the parents had to give an adopted son an inheritance, no matter how many children they already had:

> Even if Hillalum [the father] and Alittum [the mother] have many sons, Yahatti-Il [the adopted son] is the heir [to their estate], and he shall take two shares from the estate of Hillalum, his father. His younger brothers shall divide the remaining estate in equal parts. A claimant who raises a claim against him infringes on the taboo of [the sun-god] Shamash.[21]

Adoption and the laws and contracts it entailed ensured that one's family line would survive if there were no natural children or said offspring died young. They also helped maintain existing family and social customs in a society that honored tradition and witnessed very minimal change from one century to another.

Chapter Three

LIFE IN THE COMMUNITY

For an ancient Sumerian, Babylonian, Assyrian, or Persian, community life involved many of the same activities that go on in modern towns and cities. People took part in public worship, for instance. During religious festivals they either marched in or watched sacred processions and attended feasts, all intended to honor one or more gods. People also bought (or if they were merchants, sold) food, clothes, pottery vessels, utensils, jewelry, and other goods in markets or shops. In addition, a person went to the marketplace to borrow money from the ancient equivalent of a banker. (One commodity sold in these markets that fortunately is not available in modern ones was slaves.) Other common community activities in ancient Mesopotamian towns included digging wells and irrigation canals to maintain or expand local water supplies; working on state building projects, such as erecting palaces and temples; and going to court or attending public executions of convicted criminals.

Merchants and Their Wares

Among the more visible members of Mesopotamian community life were merchants. They existed in the area well before the Sumerians arrived in the mid- to late fourth millennium B.C. However, large-scale trading, buying, and selling came about only with the rise of the Sumerian cities in southern Mesopotamia. Simply put, urban centers had large numbers of residents, who needed and demanded to purchase a wide variety of goods.

Two major kinds or groups of merchants provided these goods. The members of the first group were long-range traders who obtained goods from foreign cities or nations (by exchanging goods

Honest vs. Dishonest Merchants

A surviving hymn to Shamash, patron god of merchants, describes the difference between disreputable and reputable business practices by ancient Mesopotamian merchants.

The merchant who practices trickery as he holds the corn measure . . . the curse of the people will overtake him before his time. If he demanded repayment [of a loan] before the agreed date, there will be guilt before him. His heir will not assume control of his property. [In contrast] the honest merchant who weighs out loans [fairly], thus multiplying kindness, is pleasing to Shamash, and he will prolong his life. He [the merchant] will enlarge his family, gain wealth, and like the water of a never failing spring, [his] descendants will never fail.

Quoted in W.G. Lambert, *Babylonian Wisdom Literature.* Oxford: Oxford University Press, 1960, p. 133.

made in Mesopotamia for foreign-made goods). By 3000 B.C., the Persian Gulf, Indian Ocean, and Red Sea had become lanes of sea commerce that brought foreign merchandise to cities in the Tigris-Euphrates valley. In those days Ur was situated near the shores of the Persian Gulf, so it became the main hub of trading activity in the region.[22] Merchants sailed from that city into the gulf, through what is now the Strait of Hormuz, and into the Indian Ocean. From there, they accessed markets in southern India, along the southern coasts of the Arabian peninsula, and on Africa's eastern coast. They also sailed north into the Red Sea and traded goods in Egypt. Meanwhile, other merchants traveled overland to trade with cities in Syria, Palestine, Anatolia (what is now Turkey), and other areas west of Mesopotamia. Internal trade within Mesopotamia itself used both river-based shipping and land-based donkey caravans.

The other major group of merchants were somewhat equal to today's retailers. Some bought imported goods from traders and sold them in markets and shops in Mesopotamian cities. Other retailers bought goods grown or made locally and sold them. And still others were local growers or manufacturers who sold their own products directly to the public.

Therefore, a typical open-air marketplace in an ancient Mesopotamian town featured several kinds of merchants. One thing they all had in common was their use of standardized, or universally accepted, weights and measures. Different cities, regions, and nations had differing counting and measuring systems. So a measure of wheat in Ur might be larger or smaller than one from Mari or from distant Syria. Using several different measuring systems in a single marketplace would obviously be confusing and make it easy for sellers to cheat customers. It was customary, therefore, for merchants to carry and use standard weights (objects that local officials certified as weighing a certain amount). The weights of any and all goods could be compared to these standard weights, ensuring fairness.

Merchants who sold their wares in the formal setting of a town marketplace were not the only ones who used standard weights. Small-scale, roving merchants similar to modern door-to-door salespeople were also expected to carry them. According to Nemet-Nejat:

These merchants sold to individuals, as [ancient texts make] reference to "a merchant's leather bag for weights." Dishonest practices by retail merchants were alluded to as "who, as he holds the balance [measuring scale], indulges in cheating by substituting weights." As for peddlers, the "firewood man" was noted in Assyria[n texts] and a "salt man" in Babylonia. Both could be house-to-house small traders.[23]

If standard weights and the officials who certified them looked after the public good, the merchants themselves had to provide for their own safety and welfare. To this end they created guild-like organizations, each called a *karum*. Such an organization was a sort of mutual aid society. Members helped one another guard caravans from bandits; find financial backers for big trading expeditions; and negotiate with local officials in financial matters, including how trade goods would be taxed.

Going Shopping

By the advent of the second millennium B.C., the products that Mesopotamian merchants brought to and sold in local markets were a diverse mix of local and imported items. Local farmers grew and sold barley, emmer wheat, and other grains, for instance. Mesopotamian fields (which overall were a good deal more fertile than those in modern Iraq) also yielded sesame seeds, nuts, and many vegetables including onions, garlic, cucumbers, carrots, and radishes. Among the locally grown fruits available in markets were apricots, dates, quinces, figs, cherries, and plums. A number of textiles, embroidered garments, leather goods, bronze weapons, and jewelry items were also manufactured and sold locally.

Shoppers in Ur, Sippur, Ashur, and other cities in the Tigris-Euphrates valley also found many foreign-made products to choose from. There were items made of gold, copper, ivory, pearls, and diorite (a hard, black stone) that came from Arabia and Africa's eastern coast. From farther north, in Palestine and Syria, came cedar and other hardwoods and fragrant oils and perfumes. Even farther north, Anatolia supplied tin for making bronze objects sold in Mesopotamian cities. (Bronze was made by mixing tin with copper in ratios of from six to ten parts copper to one part tin.) In addition, what is now Afghanistan was the major source of lapis lazuli, a highly prized stone with an intense bluish hue. Shoppers in Ur and Ashur could also purchase tasty wines and fine pottery containers made in faraway Greece and Cyprus (a large island in the eastern Mediterranean Sea).

Barter, Coins, and Banking

To buy these and other goods, shoppers participated in barter, the process of paying for an item with an item of equal value. In the late third millennium B.C., various Sumerian officials assigned values to agricultural products such as wheat and rye and luxury goods such as gold and hardwood furniture. These values were based on the accepted existing value of silver. Thus, when someone went to buy something, the product

Items made from materials not found in ancient Mesopotamia, such as this gold cup found in a royal tomb in Ur, were brought to the region by importers and made available in local markets.

Coins were first used in ancient Mesopotamia in the seventh century B.C. These bronze coins depicting the profile of a king date from the second century A.D.

and the item that would be exchanged for it were weighed. And their values were determined based on given weights of silver. Officials in royal palaces and major religious temples collected and stored the silver and certified that it had been weighed properly.

In fact silver became the universal standard of value in the region. "Even the value of gold was expressed in terms of the more common metal, silver," says Bertman. "In terms of relative value, first came gold (8 to 15 times more valuable than silver by weight); then silver; next lead; then copper; and finally iron, which became a common metal only in the first millennium B.C."[24]

Barter continued as the standard method for financial transactions in Mesopotamia well into the first millennium B.C. The use of coins, which were invented in Lydia (in Anatolia), did not begin in the Tigris-Euphrates region until shortly before 600 B.C. Even then, for awhile they were exchanged mostly among merchants and shopkeepers and took awhile to catch on with shoppers. In the words of University of Oklahoma scholar Daniel C. Snell, at first "coinage did not drive out other forms of money." However, gradually "coins began to be accepted." This was perhaps less because they were convenient and easy to use and more because of their political value to the cities and kings that issued them. "The city that could issue its own coinage," Snell points out, "was asserting its [financial], if not political, independence, and its designs [stamped on the front and back of the coins] could tout its own traditions."[25]

The first major Mesopotamian ruler to recognize coins as a potent political tool

Sumerian Entrepreneurs

Today entrepreneurs, people who organize and take the risks involved in business ventures, are common, respected, and even envied in Western societies. Some such wheeler-dealers also existed in ancient Mesopotamia. Evidence shows that Dumuzi-gamil, a citizen of the Sumerian city of Ur in the second millennium B.C., and a partner borrowed a large amount of silver from some wealthy merchants. The interest rate was high—23.9 percent. But the borrowers were still able to make a hefty profit for themselves by investing the money in various activities. They started selling bread to a local temple estate, for example. They also obtained contracts to sell both bread and meat to the local palace. And they took part of their profits from these ventures and lent them out to people at interest rates approaching 30 percent. In this way, Dumuzi-gamil and his partner got rich by wisely investing, rather than simply spending, the money they had borrowed.

was Darius I (reigned ca. 522–486 B.C.), the third king of the Persian Empire. He issued silver coins known as *darics*, which may have been named for him. The Greek kings who ruled Mesopotamia after Alexander the Great conquered Persia (in the late fourth century B.C.) also issued coins on a large scale.

Because coins were easy to store, carry, and exchange and had standard values, they made banking transactions simpler; so bankers became more common in Mesopotamian community life beginning in the fifth century B.C. These bankers were persons or groups who charged a fee for exchanging one form of currency for another. They also loaned out money, as did some institutions, including large temples. The money lenders usually charged interest, which could be high by today's standards—between 20 and 33 percent. At such rates, a banker could make three times as much as he initially loaned out in only a few years.

Not surprisingly, such practices made some bankers very rich. And they often passed their profession and wealth on to their children. In this way, a few large families came to dominate the banking industry in Persian- and Greek-ruled Mesopotamia. These included the Egibi of Babylon, the Ea-iluta-bani of Borsippa, and the Murashu of Nippur.

A person seeking a loan who approached such a banking firm was required to draw up a contract carved on a clay tablet. Listed was the amount borrowed, the names of the lender and borrower, the duration of the loan, the manner in which the borrower would pay it back, and other relevant information. Both parties signed the contract, and a third party witnessed it. Later, after the borrower had made all his payments, the banker handed him the contract, signifying that the debt had been paid.

Community Water Supplies

Ancient Mesopotamians borrowed money from bankers for many and different reasons, as people do today. For instance, it was common for farmers to borrow money for a few months to cover their personal expenses until they could harvest their crops and sell them at market. Even with a hefty loan, however, an individual farmer could not afford to pay for the building of the irrigation canals he needed to ensure the growth of his crops. (Large-scale irrigation to supplement normal rainfall became common in Babylonia and Sumer, in southern Mesopotamia; it was far less common in Assyria, in the north, where rainfall was more abundant.)

Indeed, such canals were large-scale community projects that only governments or other big institutions (such as

A relief from the palace of King Ashurbanipal depicts the city of Madaktu surrounded by canals. In ancient Mesopotamia, the digging and maintenance of canals was critical to growing successful crops.

temple estates) could afford to build. The importance of these waterways to the Sumerians and Babylonians is illustrated by a traditional curse these peoples passed from one generation to another: "May your canal become choked with debris!" A ruler who neglected the existing canals was likely to make his subjects unhappy and ripe for rebellion. So most kings viewed digging and maintaining canals a major priority. This explains why the famous Babylonian lawgiver and conqueror Hammurabi devoted most of the last nine years of his reign to building canals.

In the digging of a canal, thousands of tons of earth and debris had to be moved by hand, a job that could be accomplished only by large numbers of workers. Sometimes the builder used slaves. But the majority of laborers on these and other state-sponsored projects were free people who did the work to pay off part or all of their taxes.

Another way the ancient Mesopotamians acquired life-giving water was to build aqueducts. An aqueduct is an artificial channel that carries water from one location to another, usually (but not always) underground through an exca-

Dwindling Water Supplies

In the third, second, and early first millennia B.C., canals, wells, aqueducts, and cisterns provided the inhabitants of ancient Mesopotamia with considerable amounts of fresh water. This supported large local populations and helped grow huge quantities of crops. In contrast, modern Iraq has far less water and arable land and must import much of its food. One reason that much of the region became drier and less productive over time is chronic neglect.

The Babylonians, Assyrians, Persians, and Greeks carefully maintained, and at times expanded, the canals and other water facilities created by the Sumerians. Beginning in the late first millennium B.C., however, the Parthians (who had replaced the Greeks in the region) allowed these facilities to deteriorate. The next empire in the area—that of the Sassanians—spent most of its money and resources in Iran and allowed the Mesopotamian canals and aqueducts to disintegrate even further. Human wars also took a toll, as various foreign conquerors destroyed the canals as a way to defeat their enemies. In addition, nature slowly but surely erased most of what was left of Mesopotamia's ancient waterworks. The local rivers periodically changed course, leaving formerly moist areas dry. And silt and vegetation clogged water gates, canals, and wells, which steadily disappeared beneath the dust and sands.

vated tunnel. The first underground aqueducts in Mesopotamia were built by the Assyrian monarch Sargon II (ca. 721–705 B.C.). Following Assyria's fall, the Persians expanded the Assyrian system of aqueducts. The Persians called an aqueduct a *kariz.* But the term *qanat,* coined by the Arabs much later, became more widespread and remains in use today. Like canals, aqueducts were huge projects that required the labor of hundreds or even thousands of members of local communities.

Community Justice

Whether they lived in towns or in the countryside, or worked as farmers, merchants, or laborers on state building projects, all members of the community were expected to respect the local laws. Those that did not were subject to the scorn of their neighbors and swift penalties given out by local elders, town officials, or local courts. Leick describes these courts and how they operated:

> Judges could be chosen from the local community or be appointed by the king. Affected parties [the accuser, or plaintiff, and the accused, or defendant] represented their own case and brought witnesses as appropriate. Proceedings, or at least the verdicts, were written down, and numerous tablets [bearing these verdicts] have been preserved from most [ancient] historical periods. . . . Defendants

Justice in Babylonia was determined according to King Hammurabi's law code, which is collected on a stele (stone marker) from the eighteenth century B.C.

and plaintiffs were made to swear an oath on the divine emblems, such as a sun disk, which represented the god of justice, Shamash.[26]

If the defendant in a case was found guilty, his punishment varied somewhat, depending on the time and place. Sumerian courts and laws often forced the guilty person to repay his victim in some way. A monetary payment, either of silver or valuable goods, was common. The death penalty was used mainly for very serious crimes, such as rape or murder.

Centuries later, Babylonian justice seems to have been a good deal more unforgiving. Hammurabi's law code (dating from about 1750 B.C.), for example, lists many harsh punishments, perhaps based on the theory that these would deter crime. And the familiar passage about crime and punishment from the biblical book of Leviticus was influenced by Babylonian legal customs of the first millennium B.C.: "When a man causes a disfigurement in his neighbor, as he has done, it shall be done to him; fracture for fracture, eye for eye, tooth for tooth, as he has disfigured a man he shall be disfigured. He who kills [a] man shall be put to death."[27]

Indeed, in ancient Babylonia the death penalty could be imposed for theft and other minor crimes. King Ammi-saduqa, one of Hammurabi's immediate successors, issued a decree calling for the execution of corrupt government officials and merchants who cheated their customers. Punishments under ancient Assyria's justice system were also harsh and frequently cruel by modern standards. A woman who committed theft, for instance, might have her ears or nose cut off. And a man who committed adultery could be castrated and have his face sliced to shreds. Whether or not the Babylonian and Assyrian brand of justice actually deterred crime is unknown. But the fact of its harshness shows how serious these peoples were about trying to maintain community standards, obedience to authority, and public order and morality.

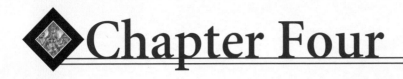

Chapter Four

SLAVES AND SERFS

Slavery was an ever-present reality of both home and community life in ancient Mesopotamia. Indeed the Sumerians, Babylonians, Assyrians, Persians, and all the other peoples who inhabited the region in antiquity owned and exploited slaves. Yet slaves, whom the Babylonians called *wardum,* were not a major part of society; rather they were useful and convenient, though not absolutely necessary, to most of their owners. (In comparison, ancient Rome was hugely dependent on slave labor at all social levels.)

Modern scholars are unsure about when slavery began in Mesopotamia and other parts of the Near East. But it is likely that the Ubaidians, who occupied the area before the Sumerians arrived, did keep at least some slaves. This is because the practice was apparently already well established in the early Sumerian period.

Initially most slaves were people taken captive in raids into the mountains lying along Mesopotamia's northern and western borders. For that reason the earliest Sumerian word for a slave translated literally as "man from the mountains." In the late third millennium (the 2000s) B.C., for instance, the Akkadian king Rimush took some four thousand prisoners during a raid into Syria. All of these captives became slaves.

Jobs and the Status of Slaves

Most of Rimush's war captives spent the rest of their lives laboring on state building projects. In other words, they dug canals or made, hauled, stacked, and decorated palaces, temples, and the outer defensive walls of cities. The government set up inexpensive housing near the work sites for these public slaves to live in. Over time other public slaves worked

A relief depicts numerous slaves on a building project engaged in heavy labor. Slaves in ancient Mesopotamia also worked in homes or on farms.

on the large estates run by the palaces and temples, doing jobs such as cleaning; assisting craftspeople and scribes; feeding sheep, cattle, and other animals; and so forth.

Still, as was also true in ancient Egypt, these unfree laborers did not do all of society's menial work. Instead they merely supplemented free workers. Most large-scale public labor in Mesopotamia was performed by free people, particularly farmers who worked part-time for the government in the months between planting and harvesting. Thus a large amount of the region's agricultural workforce always remained free.

Another group of slaves might be termed "domestic," or "household," because they worked in the homes or on the lands of private citizens. It is uncertain how many slaves existed in an average Mesopotamian household. Poor people likely had no slaves at all, because they lacked the resources to buy and maintain them. In contrast, a home owner of average means in Babylonia or Assyria in the first millennium B.C. kept maybe one, two, or three slaves. And a wealthy person in the same era had perhaps thirty, forty, or more slaves.

Household slaves did a wide variety of tasks. They cooked, cleaned, ran errands, did yard or farm work, and/or helped raise the master's children. In addition, some private owners trained their more trustworthy slaves to work in shops as clerks, textile makers, or even as secretaries. The latter probably learned to read and write, which put them in a socially uncertain position. Their status was higher than that of slaves who performed only menial labor, but lower than free, highly educated scribes.

In fact the social status of slaves in Mesopotamian society was further complicated by several factors. These factors were addressed in some of the law codes set down by Sumerian and Babylonian kings. King Hammurabi's list of laws, for instance, made several mentions of the

An Unhappy Slave Sale

Like slaves in all places and times, those in ancient Mesopotamia had many reasons to be unhappy besides their lack of freedom. One was when a slave who had settled into a house and come to feel like part of the family was then suddenly sold to another owner. In his book about life in the ancient Near East, University of Oklahoma scholar Daniel C. Snell notes the surviving record of a female slave named Usatusa and reconstructs what the master may have said to her shortly before her departure.

I sold you and your family some time ago, with the understanding that you be delivered later, when I could more easily spare you. You knew long ago that this day would come. And here it is. This is happening all over the place, people scaling back their staffs, and you shouldn't be surprised. . . . If you want to tell me about how you suckled my father and that sort of stuff, that is all very well, but a deal is a deal. I needed the money back when I made it, and I'm going to carry it through now, no matter what you want.

Daniel C. Snell, *Life in the Ancient Near East, 3100–332 B.C.* New Haven: Yale University Press, 1998, p. 66.

harsh custom of debt slavery. If a person owed a creditor a large sum of money and had no way to pay it back, he might sell himself, or his children, or even his entire family to the creditor. The debtor (or debtors) would continue to work as slaves for a set period as a substitute for the money owed. One of Hammurabi's laws named the terms and periods of enslavement involved in such an arrangement:

> If any one fail to meet a claim for debt, and sell himself, his wife, his son, and daughter for money or give them away to forced labor, they shall work for three years in the house of the man who bought them, or the proprietor, and in the fourth year they shall be set free.[28]

This shows that some people in Mesopotamia were slaves only on a temporary basis.

It appears that now and then debt slavery became so prevalent in a given community or kingdom that the ruler (or rulers) felt it made society less stable and rebellion more likely. So they declared amnesties in which they freed many or all debt slaves. In Babylonia in the early second millennium B.C., such an amnesty was called a *mesharum*, meaning "justice" or "righteousness."

Other Avenues to Slavery

The ancient law codes and other surviving evidence indicate that taking war

A contract describing the purchase of a slave by Prince Lugal-Ushumagal of Lagash is written in cuneiform on a clay tablet from 2250 B.C.

captives and selling oneself into bondage were not the only avenues to slavery. It was also possible for children who were born free to become slaves when their parents voluntarily gave them away. This usually happened only during a severe famine, when the parents could no longer afford to feed all their offspring. One solution was to send one or more of the children to a temple, where they did menial tasks for the priests and overseers. In Babylonia during the first millennium B.C., such temple slaves became an economically important social subclass. And some of them rose to hold important administrative jobs in the temples.

Still another way that people became slaves was by being born into the slavery institution. The sad reality is that slaves were viewed first and foremost as property, and as such their owners could pass them along from one generation to the next. Moreover, any child born of a slave mother and slave father was also a slave. If one or the other parent was a free person, however, the situation was quite different. According to another of Hammurabi's laws: "If a state [i.e., public] slave or the slave of a free man marry the daughter of a free man, and children are born, the master of the slave shall have no right to enslave the children of the free."[29]

Various ancient Mesopotamian laws and customs protected not only the children of free people, but also the slave masters themselves. Indeed a slave owner enjoyed certain protections even when buying a slave. One Babylonian law provided that purchasing a slave included a thirty-day warranty. That is,

Free-Born Women Who Married Slaves

In a society in which slaves lived in the same houses as their masters and some slaves bore children by their masters, it was necessary to have laws covering the legal status and economic rights of all involved. One of Hammurabi's more complex laws protected the inheritance of a free-born woman who married a slave (if and after the slave died):

[I]f] a State slave or the slave of a freedman marry a man's [free-born] daughter, and after he marries her she bring a dowry from [her] father's house, if then they both enjoy it and found a household, and accumulate means, if then the slave die, then she who was free born may take her dowry, and all that her husband and she had earned; she shall divide them into two parts, one-half the master for the slave shall take, and the other half shall the free-born woman take for her children. If the free-born woman had no gift [dowry] she shall take all that her husband and she had earned and divide it into two parts; and the master of the slave shall take one-half and she shall take the other for her children.

Quoted in "The Code of Hammurabi." www.wsu.edu/~dee/MESO/CODE.HTM.

if the slave became seriously ill during the thirty days following the sale, the new owner could return him or her and get his money back in full.

The law also protected masters for "damages" suffered by their slaves. Another of Hammurabi's laws stated: "If [a free person] puts out the eye of a man's slave, or breaks the bone of a man's slave, he shall pay [the owner] one-half of [the slave's] value." Thus, rather unfairly by modern standards, if someone hurt a slave, the master, not the slave, received sympathy and compensation. Similarly, another law protected the master against "malpractice" by doctors who might treat an injured slave: "If a physician makes a large incision in the slave of a free man, and kill him, he shall replace the slave with another slave."[30]

Treatment of Slaves

The law also often dictated how slaves should or could be treated or punished in various situations. There were certain written laws and penalties for the case of a runaway slave, for instance. Escape attempts by slaves in ancient Mesopotamia were probably fairly uncommon, partly because punishments for runaways were usually harsh. An escaped slave might have been beaten severely or starved for several days or longer. It was also common for the master to use a red-hot iron rod to brand the word for "escaped slave" onto the runaway's forehead. Usually the owner did not kill the

escapee. This is because the slave was still a valuable piece of property, and buying new slaves to replace those slain in anger was financially unsound.

Another reason that slaves rarely tried to escape was society's attitude toward slavery. The vast majority of people viewed it as a natural and inevitable condition that even the gods excused. So they had little or no sympathy for the escapee and refused to give him or her shelter. Those few who did feel compassion for the runaways faced severe penalties if they aided them. Hammurabi's sixteenth law stated: "If any one receive into his house a runaway male or female slave of the court, or of a freedman [freed slave], and does not [report it to the authorities], the master of the house shall be put to death." Law number 19 was equally harsh: "If he hold the slaves in his house, and they are caught there, he shall be put to death."[31] A third law dealing with runaways targeted barbers who shaved off the long locks of hair that often designated slave status in Mesopotamia. Any barber convicted of this offense could have his hand cut off.

Conversely, by law people who returned escaped slaves to their masters were rewarded, as shown in another Babylonian law: "If any one find runaway male or female slaves in the open country and bring them to their masters, the master of the slaves shall pay him two shekels of silver."[32] Also, to help single out escapees from ordinary people, slaves were routinely marked in some way. Sometimes, noted scholar H.W.F. Saggs writes,

A relief shows King Sennacherib being fanned by a pair of slaves while on his throne at a military camp. Slaves in ancient Mesopotamia served both royals and private citizens.

they were made to wear "a characteristic hairdo." Many other slaves were branded with a hot iron, like cattle. In such cases, the owner's mark, or for a temple slave the god's symbol, was burnt on the slave's hand or wrist. There was no compassion for age or gender, and in [Babylonia in the first millennium B.C.] we meet a six-year-old slave girl whose wrist was marked with the names of her two owners.[33]

Running away was not the only reason that a slave could be punished or otherwise mistreated. Newly captured slaves were often resistant and unruly. And it was common practice to put them in neck stocks—wooden restraints that painfully restricted their movement—day and night until they calmed down.

In extreme cases, an unmanageable slave might be blinded to make him or her easier to handle.

Slaves' Rights and Privileges

So far the picture sketched of the lives of ancient Babylonian slaves appears grim at best. Alleviating slaves' miserable condition somewhat, however, was the fact that they had a few rights and privileges. First, household slaves frequently developed close relationships with the master and his family members. And if the master had no children of his own (or his children had died), he might legally adopt one or more of his more trusted slaves. This act was partly selfish in that it assured the slave owner that he would have someone to take care of him in his old age.

Another situation that allowed some slaves to better their condition was when the master's wife was physically unable to bear children. In such a case, the owner might select a slave woman to bear his child. If the master then legally adopted the child, that child would not only be a free person, but also eligible to inherit part of the father's estate when he died. According to one of Hammurabi's laws:

If his wife bear sons to a man, or his maid-servant have borne sons, and the father while still living says to the children whom his maid-servant has borne: "My sons," and he count them with the sons of his wife; if then the father die, then the sons of the wife and of the maid-servant shall divide the paternal property in common.[34]

Of course if the father did not legally adopt the child, the child was not entitled to share in the inheritance. But on the positive side, he or she could no longer be enslaved, as decreed in Hammurabi's law number 171:

If, however, the father while still living did not say to the sons of the maid-servant: "My sons," and then the father dies, then the sons of the maid-servant shall not share with the sons of the wife, but the freedom of the maid and her sons shall be granted. The sons of the wife shall have no right to enslave the sons of the maid.[35]

It is likely that in many such situations, the child's biological mother was freed as a reward for the services she had performed for the family.

Another privilege enjoyed by some ancient Mesopotamian slaves was working in a shop or other business concern (usually, though not always, owned by the master). Such a slave received small but regular wages for his or her efforts. Some evidence suggests that at least a few working slaves saved up a considerable amount of money over time. It remains unclear whether they could use this money to buy their freedom, as ancient Roman slaves could. What is

Slaves of Former Slaves

In the ancient world, including Mesopotamia, slavery was seen as a natural, inevitable situation. So even many former slaves, or freedmen, routinely bought slaves of their own. And a number of laws evolved to protect freedmen from injury, at the hands of both slaves and free-born people. Hammurabi's Babylonian law code included these examples:

If the slave of a freedman strike the body of a freedman, his ear shall be cut off. If [a free-born man] put out the eye of a freedman, or break the bone of a freedman, he shall pay one gold mina. If he knock out the teeth of a freedman, he shall pay one-third of a gold mina.

Quoted in "The Code of Hammurabi." www.wsu.edu/~dee/MESO/CODE.HTM.

more certain is that a few slaves did, by various means, gain their freedom and went on to become successful businesspeople. This shows that a considerable amount of upward mobility existed in ancient Mesopotamian society. In other words, people born in poverty, slavery, or some other lowly situation might, under the right circumstances, significantly improve their financial condition and social status.

Mesopotamian Serfs

The many and diverse social situations and laws dealing with slavery in ancient Mesopotamia were further complicated by the existence of a second class of unfree people. Most modern experts refer to them as "serfs" (although some prefer the term *villeins*). As in medieval Europe, Mesopotamian serfs were mostly peasants, or low-class, poor agricultural laborers. Strictly speaking they were not slaves, so they could not be sold along with land; yet financially they were almost completely dependent on the wealthy individuals or institutions who owned the land. (The main social institutions that employed serfs were the large estates run by the palaces and temples.) In other words, legally serfs were free to leave. But they were too poor to own land of their own, so they saw no other choice but to stay, work for, and largely do the bidding of their employers.

One might become a serf in ancient Mesopotamia in one of several ways. According to Saggs, some serfs were

descendants of earlier free citizens who had lost some of their rights in consequence of economic adversity [hard times]. Others were [originally] foreign immigrants, prisoners of war who had not become

A relief shows a man, possibly a serf, tending to a plant near a palm tree. Serfs in Mesopotamia were peasants, poor laborers who were free citizens but economically tied to their work tending the fields of wealthy landowners.

slaves, fugitives from some other city-state, and society's rejects, such as widows and orphans. Often their economic circumstances were no better than those of slaves.[36]

Serfs may have existed in small numbers in Sumerian times (the third millennium B.C.), but it was in the first few centuries of the second millennium B.C. that the region's rulers and their laws began to recognize this special class of workers. Hammurabi, for example, called them *mushkenum,* from a word meaning "one who prostrates himself [bows low]." The exact situation of serfs in this period is unclear. But it appears that, like medieval serfs, they kept part of the food they grew for themselves and gave up the rest to the landowners.

By the start of the first millennium B.C., the *mushkenum* seemed to have merged, more or less, with the mass of ordinary free Mesopotamian workers. Yet serflike laborers still existed. The large estates run by well-to-do Assyrians, Persians, and Parthians all employed them. The fact is that poverty was an ever-present reality in the ancient and medieval worlds. And at any given time, varying numbers of free people were so desperate that they became little better than slaves.

Chapter Five

GAMES, SPORTS, AND TRAVEL

Most people in the ancient world, including Mesopotamia, were poor or of little more than modest means. So out of necessity they had to work most days of the week and usually put in long hours by modern standards. This left little time for leisure activities. Yet like people in all ages and places, they did entertain themselves with games and sports when they could. And the nobles and other wealthy folk, of course, were able to devote even more time to such activities. Some of these games and sporting events are still popular across the world today.

Travel was another way to break up the monotony of work and daily routines. However, for much of Mesopotamia's ancient period, there was very little of the vacation-oriented travel or tourism that is so popular today. Most Sumerians, Babylonians, and Persians who took long trips beyond the Tigris-Euphrates valley were traders, soldiers, and official messengers. They brought back tales of the foreign sights they had seen to those who lacked the means to travel. Still, some long-range tourism did eventually develop in the ancient Near East. Tourists have been documented in Egypt (visiting the pyramids and Great Sphinx) as early as the second millennium B.C. And the Greek historian Herodotus (among others) toured both Egypt and Mesopotamia in the fifth century B.C.

From Gambling to Board Games

For the vast majority of ancient Mesopotamians who had to entertain themselves in their native communities, gambling was always a favorite pastime. The Sumerians, Babylonians, and Persians all pursued various forms of gambling, especially dice games. The dice they used were somewhat different from modern versions. First, many ancient dice featured four triangular-shaped surfaces, rather than the six square-shaped surfaces common in modern dice. The values and meaning of the throws were also sometimes different. The number seven was not necessarily important or lucky to Mesopotamian dice throwers, for instance. In addition, they did not play for money until coins came into wide use in the mid-first millennium B.C. (Before that, people wagered goods, such as sheep, horses, clothes, weapons, and so forth.)

The remains of a game board and pieces were found in the excavation of a royal cemetery in Ur. Dice and boards discovered in various ruins indicate that ancient Mesopotamians enjoyed games in their leisure time.

Dice were, as they are today, also used in board games. Modern excavators discovered the remains of a Sumerian board game in the royal cemetery at Ur. Dating to the early third millennium B.C., the game was similar in some ways to the ancient Egyptian game *senet,* which came into use later. The surviving Mesopotamian version is made of wood covered by layers of small pieces of white shell, lapis lazuli, and red limestone. It measures about 5 inches by 11 inches (13cm by 28cm) and has twenty-one squares, a large rectangular zone, a small rectangular zone, and a narrow bridge connecting the two zones. Each player possessed seven tokens, or playing pieces. It remains uncertain exactly how the game was played.

The ancient Persians, who controlled Mesopotamia two millennia after the Sumerians did, played some board games fairly similar to popular modern ones. One was an early form of chess, called *shatrang.* It featured a chessboard like today's version and playing pieces representing military personnel and weapons. The Persians also played a form of backgammon, called *nard,* described by scholar Norman B. Hunt:

> The Persians used conical stones as counters and two dice. The coun-

Ancient Persian Polo

The ancient Persians played an early form of polo. No detailed ancient accounts have survived. But a medieval Persian poet, Hakeem Ferdosi, included a brief description of a game, still played as it had been centuries before, in his ninth-century epic, the Shahnameh.

Afrasiab started the game by hitting the ball first. At once, drumbeats of a band started and the spectators began a festive frenzy of dancing and clapping to encourage the sides. [The great hero] Siavash skillfully controlled the ball and, before it fell to the ground, he hit the ball so hard that it disappeared from view. Afrasiab and his team were startled by such power and skill and hit another ball. Again, Siavash hit the ball hard and caused a stir. The spectators, who were impressed by his ability, began to cheer him on. Afrasiab and Siavash then let their men continue the game while they watched from golden thrones. The Iranians were dominating the game. Siavash, who was witnessing the humiliation of the Turanians, told his men . . . to be good guests and consider that this was only a game of polo and not war. Following Siavash's wish, his men let their hosts win the game on their home turf.

Shahmaneh: The Persian Book of Kings. New York: Viking, 2006, p. 269.

A relief depicts a royal lion hunt. Hunting for sport was a popular pursuit for kings and other wealthy men in ancient Mesopotamia.

ters could only move along marked squares in a forward direction, with the figures of one player moving in a clockwise direction and those of the opponent anti-clockwise. The rules were phrased in typical military terminology. Each player pursued and outwitted his opponent by forcing him into a fight where his counters were outmaneuvered and "killed"—forced off the board.[37]

Outdoor Sports

Games that were more physical than board games and played outdoors were also popular in ancient Mesopotamia. Sport hunting was a well-known example, in part because it was practiced mainly by wealthy men, particularly kings. Members of this elite group were the only ones who could afford to mount elaborate expeditions involving horses, chariots, traps, corrals, wagons, and dozens of helpers. Evidence shows that the Assyrian king Tiglath-pileser I (reigned ca. 1115–1077 B.C.) hunted tigers, leopards, lions, bears, hyenas, bison, deer, wild pigs, gazelle, onagers (wild asses), elephants, and ostriches. He also claimed to have caught a *nahiru,* possibly a dolphin or whale, in the waters of the Mediterranean Sea. Another Assyrian king, Ashurnasirpal II (ca. 884–859 B.C.), boasted that he slew thirty elephants, along with hundreds of lions and wild oxen. One reason for these large numbers of dead animals may have been that royal hunts were often staged events. Professional trappers collected the animals and put them in enclosed areas, where the king hunted them with minimal difficulty.

These royal hunts also had religious overtones. In the symbolic sense they were seen as a way for the king, as a human champion of the gods, to help his subjects. Leick explains that a royal lion hunt

> was a public performance of the ancient duties of the king, to protect his subjects from evil. The symbolic connection was underlined by the fact that the hunt took place at the time of the New Year festival, when the king was acting out a number of [religious] roles.[38]

Another vigorous outdoor game played in ancient Mesopotamia was polo, the oldest-known team sport. Its exact origins are unclear. But the Persians were playing it at least as early as 600 B.C. The third Persian king, Darius I (ca. 522–486 B.C.), promoted it as a way to improve the horse-riding skills of his cavalrymen. At the time, each team had up to a hundred players. There were few rules or restrictions, which made matches extremely rough, resulting in serious injuries and sometimes even death. Later rulers introduced smaller teams and stricter regulations. This made the game considerably less dangerous, so kings and nobles, including some women, began playing.

Other sports that still exist today were popular among the Persians and other Mesopotamian peoples. Persian men, both rich and poor, and particularly soldiers, competed in swimming, chariot racing, horse racing, weightlifting, and archery. And both the Babylonians and Assyrians engaged in archery as well, along with horse racing.

The Always Popular Wrestling

No other game or contest was as universally popular as wrestling, which is probably the world's oldest sport. All Mesopotamians, from the Sumerians and Babylonians to the Persians, Greeks, and Sassanians, avidly pursued it. Depictions of Sumerian wrestling matches that took place circa 3000 B.C. were discovered in Iraq in the 1930s. One of these, a small bronze sculpture, shows two wrestlers grabbing hold of the wrestling belts they wore around their hips. (Wrestling belts were common among most ancient peoples and are still used by wrestlers in a number of countries today. By pulling hard on an opponent's belt, a wrestler tried to force that opponent off balance.)

A sport as popular as wrestling was bound to be described in literature. And

Assyrian Sport Archery

During their royal hunts, the ancient Assyrian kings used a variety of weapons to kill their prey. A common way to kill lions, for instance, was to shoot arrows at them. Some surviving stone sculptures from the ruins of the Assyrian city of Ninevah show King Ashurbanipal (reigned ca. 668–627 B.C.) in his chariot, bow in hand. Scholar Arthur Cotterell describes the scene:

He [Ashurbanipal] can be seen firing his bow from a heavy chariot during a lion hunt. One sculpture shows the king shooting ahead, while two guards ward off with spears a wounded lion attacking the chariot from the rear. The heroic encounter is somewhat undercut by another relief, which reveals a game-keeper about to release from a cage a captured lion. As the monarch reserved to himself the right to kill lions, they were collected in the wild and taken to the palace for royal sport.

Arthur Cotterell, *Chariot: The Astounding Rise and Fall of the World's First War Machine.* New York: Overlook, 2005, p. 240.

A section of a relief depicting a hunt led by King Ashurbanipal shows a lion that was captured specifically for the king to kill being released from a cage, thus rigging the event to ensure the king's success.

indeed, the most famous Mesopotamian literary work, the *Epic of Gilgamesh*, contains a famous example. The title character, whom ancient writers often called "Gilgamesh the wrestler," fights a rival, Enkidu (who later becomes his friend).

The knock-down, drag-out bout is reminiscent of the kind of unruly brawls seen in today's pro-wrestling matches.

There were other, more structured forms of ancient wrestling, however. Most scholars think that Babylonian

A copper sculpture shows two soldiers grappling during a wrestling match. Wrestling was a popular sport among all peoples of ancient Mesopotamia.

A relief depicts men traveling alongside a river. Transportation options in ancient Mesopotamia were limited to walking, taking boats, and using animals either to ride or to pull carts or chariots.

and Assyrian wrestlers used moves similar and sometimes identical to those of ancient Egyptian wrestlers. At Beni Hasan, on the Nile River in central Egypt, archaeologists found more than four hundred paintings showing wrestlers from the early second millennium B.C. Most of the moves and holds depicted in these paintings remain standard for modern high school, college, and Olympic wrestlers.

Travel: Forms of Transportation

Whether or not Mesopotamian wrestlers copied the moves of Egyptian wrestlers or vice versa is unknown. (The sport may well have evolved separately in each area.)

More certain is that some people, especially traders, were traveling between these regions at an early date. Also, beginning with the rise of empires in Mesopotamia in the late third millennium B.C., whole armies regularly journeyed hundreds of miles to raid or make war in Palestine, Armenia, Iran, and other places outside the Tigris-Euphrates valley.

Whether the trip was long or short, however, the means of transportation available to travelers were fairly limited and basic. People walked, rode donkeys, sat in wagons or chariots pulled by animals, or floated in small boats on the local rivers. (People in Mesopotamia did not begin traveling by horse until the late second and early first millennium B.C.; even then, there were no stirrups, which made it difficult to maintain one's balance on a horse.)

The first wagons likely appeared in Mesopotamia sometime between 3500 and 3000 B.C., when the wheel came into widespread use. These early wheels were weighty and bulky, as they were constructed of two solid half-disks of wood nailed together. The wagons were quite heavy, therefore, and required several large animals to pull them.

Centuries later, in the second millennium B.C., craftspeople learned to bend strips of wood to form the wheel rims. Renowned scholar Lionel Casson explains why this was such a crucial breakthrough. "This enabled them to replace the ponderous disk wheels of an earlier day with wheels made of spokes . . . and to replace the cart's heavy all-wood body with one of a curved wooden frame overlaid with a covering of hides or wicker."[39] The result was a much lighter, more manageable vehicle that made travel and transport faster and easier.

Travel: Roads and Lodging

Still, wagons and chariots long remained practical only for trips of fewer than a hundred or so miles. As Casson points out, this was because of a lack of good, serviceable roads:

A walker or animal needs only a track. A vehicle needs a road, and this could well have been one of the major reasons why traders did not regularly go about in carts or wagons. In this early age, there were not many routes that could take wheeled traffic. [For many centuries] even the finest of these highways offered but a bare minimum. Paving was almost non-existent. . . . War chariots rolled over the countryside on dirt roads. Bridges, too, were a rarity. There were practically none in Egypt and Mesopotamia.[40]

It was not until the first millennium B.C., that the Assyrians, and later the Persians, built systems of major roads for use by travelers, traders, messengers, and armies. Though relatively few in number, some of these roads were long and well maintained. The finest of all was the Persian royal road that ran for some 1,500 miles (2,414km) from Mesopotamia northwestward into Anatolia.

The royal road and other new Near Eastern highways could accommodate not only wagons loaded with goods, but also large numbers of troops laden down with weapons and gear. Another heavy form of traffic on the major roads was a big, expensive, luxurious traveling vehicle. The Greeks called it a *harmamaxa,* roughly translated as "chariot wagon." It was an enormous carriage with four or more massive wheels, a roof, and hanging curtains on the sides to maintain the privacy of those riding inside. It provided a fairly comfortable means of travel for those royals and nobles who could afford it.

Persia's Postal System

Among those ancient Mesopotamians who traveled long distances on a regular basis were messengers and mail carriers. No universal system of delivering letters and packages to and from ordinary people then existed. But rulers, governors, and other high officials employed riders to deliver messages, letters, and/or decrees. Assyrian rulers were the first to do this on a large scale. And their system was the basis of a more sophisticated one established by the Persians in the wake of Assyria's decline. Various ancient sources credit either the first Persian king, Cyrus II, or the third one, Darius I, with establishing the Persian postal system, called the Barid. The riders mounted their horses and sped along several long "royal roads," including one that stretched from Susa, in southeastern Mesopotamia, to Sardis, in western Anatolia. At first the Barid delivered only official government mail. But over time the riders also carried small amounts of business and personal correspondence as well, foreshadowing the more universal postal systems of the future.

Another comfort for travelers that developed along with the growing road system in the first millennium B.C. was a series of hostels. Constructed every dozen or so miles, these were places where messengers could change horses and traders and other travelers could rest, find food and water, and in some cases stay overnight. This was not a new idea. Centuries before, some Sumerian rulers had erected a few such way stations between major cities in southern Mesopotamia. Archaeologists found writings by Shulgi (ca. 2094–2047 B.C.), the second king of Ur III, bragging about how he had made travel within his kingdom easier:

I [reinforced] the roads, put in order the highways of the Land. I marked out the double-hour distances [i.e., put up road markers], and built there lodging houses. I planted gardens by their side and established resting-places. . . . Whichever direction one comes from, one can refresh oneself at their cool sides; and the traveler who reaches nightfall on the road can seek haven there as in a well-built city.[41]

None of the Sumerian hostels have survived. But modern excavators have found the remnants of a few versions built later by the Greeks and Romans when they briefly had charge of Mesopotamia. They were originally one- or two-story structures about 70 feet (21m) long and 40 feet (12m) wide. Each had a small courtyard in which to park travelers' wagons and a stable that could hold perhaps eight to twelve animals. A typical hostel/inn also featured a blacksmith's shop for repairing wagon wheels and axles, a kitchen, dining room, and a few small bedrooms for those travelers who desired to stay the night.

There was no electricity or running water in these establishments, of course, so they were not very comfortable by modern standards. Their existence, however, demonstrates that many of the basic features modern travelers enjoy were first invented in what is now Iraq more than four thousand years before the United States and other modern nations came into being.

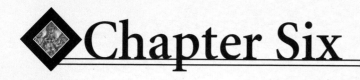
GODS AND RELIGIOUS BELIEFS

Devout religious beliefs were a major part of the lives and societies of all the peoples who lived in ancient Mesopotamia. Different peoples often had different names for the gods worshiped in the region; yet the basic images, powers, demands, and rules of these deities remained essentially the same. So one can generalize about a Mesopotamian religion or belief system broadly accepted by the Sumerians, Babylonians, and Assyrians for almost three thousand years.

Eventually the Persians and Greeks introduced somewhat different gods and beliefs into the area. Yet people's religious devotion and their belief that human morality was given and governed by the gods remained in force. Deeply ingrained in the region's belief systems, and by extension society, was the concept of right versus wrong and a sort of universal obligation for people to strive toward what was right. "The Sumerians," Kramer explains,

> cherished goodness and truth, law and order, justice and freedom [and] mercy and compassion. And they abhorred evil and falsehood [and] lawlessness and disorder. . . . Kings and rulers constantly boasted [that] they had established law and order in the land. [And] practically all the major deities . . . are extolled in Sumerian hymns as lovers of the good and just, of truth and righteousness.[42]

Thus, though not every person was honest and just, society had strict ethical norms that many people at least tried to follow. There was a strong sense of social conscience, which often translated into compassionate acts such as protecting the weak and widows and orphans.

A Prayer for Forgiveness

A number of ancient Mesopotamian prayers have survived. This Sumerian-Akkadian one asks the gods to forgive the person for some sin or other transgression:

May the fury of my lord's heart be quieted toward me. May the god who is not known be quieted toward me. May the goddess who is not known be quieted toward me. . . . In ignorance, I have eaten that forbidden by my god. In ignorance, I have set foot on that prohibited by my goddess. O Lord, my transgressions are many; great are my sins. . . . Man is dumb; he knows nothing. Mankind, everyone that exists, what does he know? Whether he is committing sin or doing good, he does not even know. . . . Remove my transgressions [and] I will sing your praise. May your heart, like the heart of a real mother, be quieted toward me.

Quoted in Ferris J. Stephens, ed., *Ancient Near Eastern Texts*. Princeton: Princeton University Press, 1950, pp. 391–92.

These and other righteous acts and concepts were often encouraged by incorporating them into the law codes issued by rulers such as Babylonia's King Hammurabi. In such ways the peoples of ancient Mesopotamia regularly channeled their devout religious beliefs into their social lives. And this long remained a crucial factor in ongoing efforts to maintain a civil and just society.

Belief in the Divine

One strong motivation for acting in a civil, just manner was the deeply felt belief that the gods were watching humanity and at any given moment might intervene to punish the wicked. The perception and images of these divinities changed considerably over time. In the prehistoric period—that is, centuries before the Sumerians introduced writing—it was widely thought that the world was alive with invisible spirits. This belief system, common to ancient peoples across the globe, is called animism. It proposes that spirits, both good and evil, inhabit the sky, mountains, rocks, trees, fields, streams, rivers, and other aspects of nature.

Eventually these nature spirits took on human form and displayed humanlike characteristics. Also the belief developed that the gods had created humanity, were keenly interested in human affairs, and had set down rules to govern both nature and the human condition. The Sumerians called these rules *me* (pronounced *may*), while the Babylonians and Assyrians called them *parsu*. According to Bertman:

The *me* defined such aspects of civilization as government and religion, war and peace, sexual intercourse (including prostitution), art and music, and crafts and professions, as well as such abstractions as truth and falsehood, and sadness and joy. The implementation of the *me* was supervised by the gods, especially by An (Akkadian Anu), the god of creation, and Enlil (Akkadian Ellil), heaven's chief executive.[43]

Another aspect of divinely inspired order accepted by Mesopotamia's early inhabitants was the so-called Tablet of Destiny. Supposedly it contained records of the future fates of both gods and humans. And anyone who held it exercised superhuman powers. (For that reason it was highly desired, and several myths described attempts to steal it.)

Still another aspect of belief in the divine order was the concept of the personal god. It was thought that this deity watched over a person and that he or she could pray to it anytime and anywhere. The manner in which one chose a personal god is unclear. But it is known that some gods were patrons, or protectors, of farmers, others of soldiers, and still others of craftspeople. A personal god could also be the patron deity of a town or city. Such a god was thought to have a special interest in the city and its people and to watch over them.

Major and Minor Gods

Some of these local gods eventually gained national importance. This happened first with the Sumerians, as their culture spread across southern Mesopotamia in the late fourth and early third millennia B.C. They then passed along

A kudurru (boundary stone) issued by King Melishishu II in the second millennium B.C. contains the emblems of various gods, including Anu, Enlil, Ea, Ishtar, and Shamash.

their gods, or at least the basic images and functions of these deities, to the region's later peoples. For example, the chief Sumerian god, Enlil, became the model for the leading Babylonian deity Marduk, as well as the Assyrians' supreme god, Ashur.

It was thought that Enlil (Marduk/Ashur) bestowed the gift of kingship on certain special humans. Also, the chief god brought wind and rain and thereby ensured that crops would grow. (He also sometimes unleashed torrential rains and floods to punish people.) In Mesopotamian mythology, Enlil married the goddess Ninlil, and they had several divine children—among them the sun god Utu (Shamash to the Babylonians and Assyrians), the moon god Nanna (Sin), and Inanna (Ishtar), goddess of love and sexual passion. Because he guarded the Tablet of Destiny, Enlil could "see all" and predict future events. Not surprisingly, prayers and poems glorified him with lines such as: "Enlil, whose command is far-reaching, lofty his word and holy, whose pronouncement [word] is unchangeable . . . whose lifted eye scans the lands . . . the earth-gods bow down before him [and] the heaven-gods humble themselves before him."[44]

Many people aimed equally earnest prayers at Enlil's female child Inanna. Besides love and sex, she was associated with war and seen as a protector of kings and ruling dynasties. The great conqueror Sargon of Akkad, for instance, called on her to support him in battle. Another striking image of her was her Babylonian guise as Ishtar, "Queen of Heaven," in which she was associated with the planet Venus.

Another important Sumerian god was Enki, whom the Babylonians and Assyrians worshiped as Ea. As "god of the waters," he supposedly oversaw all the waters above and below the earth. And the Tigris and Euphrates rivers were said to flow from his body. (This is why artists often showed him with springs of water flowing from his shoulders or from a vase he held in his hands.) Enki was also a god of wisdom, based on the idea that he possessed secret knowledge of magic, and the patron deity of craftspeople. Gods such as Enlil, Inanna, and Enki were seen as having human passions and shortcomings, as well as human form. Thus, as noted scholar of Mesopotamia Georges Roux puts it, "they represented the best and worst of human nature on a superhuman scale."[45]

In addition to these and other major gods, the early Mesopotamians recognized a number of minor supernatural deities and beings. Among these were the Iggigi, who had no individual names and performed menial labor for the major gods. Another group of minor gods, the Annunaki, also attended to the main gods. The fact that the Annunaki resembled the angels of the Old Testament is not a coincidence. The Hebrews who wrote it were familiar with them and in the book of Genesis called them the Jedi (or Nephilim). There were also frightening minor gods, such as the demon Pazuzu, who had a scaly body and wings.

Hymn to the Great Goddess

The ancient Mesopotamians sang hymns, just as devout people do today. This surviving example is to Inanna, goddess of love and war.

I am Inanna! Which god compares with me? [The chief god] Enlil gave me the heavens and he gave me the Earth. I am Inanna! He gave me lordship, and he gave me queenship. He gave me battles and he gave me fighting. He gave me the storm-wind and he gave me the dust cloud. He placed the heavens on my head as a crown. He put the Earth at my feet as sandals. He wrapped [a] holy [robe] around my body. He put the holy scepter in my hand. The [other] gods are [like] small birds, but I am the falcon. . . . . When I enter the Ekur, the house of Enlil, the gate-keeper does not lift his hand against my breast; the minister does not tell me,

A fertility statue from the eighteenth century B.C. is thought to be that of Inanna, the goddess of love and war.

"Rise!" The heavens are mine and the Earth is mine. I am heroic! Which god compares with me?

Quoted in Electronic Text Corpus of Sumerian Literature. http://etcsl.orinst.ox.ac.uk/cgi-bin/etcsl.cgi?text=t.4.07.6&charenc=j#.

(A statue of Pazuzu is seen in the famous 1973 film, *The Exorcist.*)

Persian Gods and Beliefs

The Persians introduced a newer faith into Mesopotamia when they conquered it in the sixth century B.C. And the Sassanians, who ruled the region from the third to seventh centuries A.D., revived the Persian religion. This does not mean that the Persians forced their faith on their Mesopotamian subjects. Persian rulers were usually tolerant of foreign cultures and beliefs and allowed most of the inhabitants of the region to

Zoroaster was a semi-mythical Iranian prophet whose followers spread their faith, known as Zoroastrianism, to Mesopotamia when it was conquered by the Persians in the sixth century B.C.

continue worshiping their traditional gods. (Some Persian kings did destroy a few temples in Mesopotamia and elsewhere. But such acts were intended to punish a certain city for disloyalty or rebellion rather than to suppress the local religion.)

The faith practiced by the Persians and those non-Persians who chose to convert to it was based on the teachings of an Iranian prophet named Zoroaster (or Zarathustra). A semi-mythical figure, he may have lived in the mid- to late second millennium B.C. He preached that an old Iranian sky god named Ahura-Mazda was the one major and true god of the universe.

Supposedly, Ahura-Mazda, who became known as the "Wise Lord," revealed to Zoroaster several truths about life and the world. Among these was that there existed (and always will exist) an ongoing struggle between good and evil. The leading fighters in this contest were forces known as "the Truth" (*Asa*) and "the Lie" (*Drug*, pronounced *droog*). Ahura-Mazda became the leading champion of truth and goodness, assisted by six or seven immortal forces, the Amesha Spenta. (In the earliest version of Zoroastrianism, the Spenta were not gods or beings, per se. Rather they were seen as manifestations, or attri-

The Prophet Zoroaster

The ancient Persians credited the founding of their faith, now called Zoroastrianism, with a prophet named Zoroaster. (They called him Zartosht; the name Zoroaster comes from the Greek corruption of Zartosht, Zorastres.) He may or may not have been a real person. If he *was* real, modern experts say the most likely era in which he lived was ca. 1400–1000 B.C.

Most of what little is known about Zoroaster's life comes from Zoroastrian writings, mainly the *Avesta* and *Gathas*. He was probably born and raised in Iran or the lands lying a bit farther east. At about the age of thirty, he had a vision of God (similar to the later visions experienced by Christianity's St. Paul and Islam's great prophet, Mohammed). In Zoroaster's case, the god was Ahura-Mazda, who went on to become the principal Persian god. Ahura-Mazda revealed certain truths to Zoroaster, including the existence of an ongoing battle between the forces of good and evil and the need for human beings to do good works. The prophet then went out and began converting people to what later became the main faith of the Persian and Sassanian empires.

butes, of Ahura-Mazda himself. One personified righteousness, another good thought, another wisdom, and so forth. Over time, however, worshipers came to see them as archangel-like assistants to the supreme deity.)

The evil opponents of Ahura-Mazda and the Spenta were led by a dark being or force called Ahriman. His wicked followers, the *daevas,* were equivalent to demons in older Mesopotamian faiths. In the words of former university of Chicago scholar A.T. Olmstead, Ahriman, the "false teacher," tries to destroy all that is proper and moral in life. "He prevents the possession of good thought [and] turns the wise into liars. He desolates the pastures and he lifts his weapons against the righteous."[46]

In the ancient Persian religion, worshipers were naturally expected to reject the evil Ahriman and his lies. Instead, they should help the poor, have good thoughts, speak good words, and practice good deeds. The penalties for not taking this upright path were severe. "All men in this world must support the good," the late, noted scholar Chester G. Starr wrote about Persian beliefs, or else be condemned to "serve the spirits of darkness. In the end would come a Last Judgment which would send the good to heaven and the bad to hell."[47] The Zoroastrian hell was called the Place of Worst Existence.

Beliefs About the Afterlife

The Persian conception of the afterlife—with a heaven where good people went after death and a hell to house the spirits of bad people—resembled that of today's Christians and Muslims. In contrast, the conception of the afterlife held by the Sumerians, Babylonians, and most other ancient Mesopotamians was considerably different. They "did not believe in either retributions or rewards for one's [earthly] behavior after death," Leick

A relief depicts two demigods on either side of the epic hero Gilgamesh, whose quest for the secret of eternal life was met with the lesson that immortality is only for the gods.

writes. "Instead, they were more inclined to interpret misfortune, illness, and of course death itself as a form of punishment for 'sin.'"[48]

It is not that these peoples felt there was no afterlife. In fact they did conceive of a place where human souls might go following death, as revealed in some of their writings. It had various names, including the "Land of the Dead," "Great Earth," or the "Land of No Return." This Underworld-like land was ruled by the goddess Ereshkigal and the god Nergal, who lived in a palace made of lapis lazuli.

The problem for most ancient Mesopotamians was their belief that when they entered this nether realm, they would not be living in the palace with the gods. Rather, they would be condemned to dwell on the dreary, gray, uninviting plains surrounding the palace. There they would simply exist, experiencing neither suffering nor joy, neither reward nor punishment. As Kramer says, "Mesopotamians believed that life in the Underworld was at best a dismal reflection of its earthly counterpart. They had little reason to expect a blissful afterlife, no matter how blameless they may have been [in their earthly lives]."[49]

Another unpleasant aspect of this view of the afterlife, for both the dead and living, was the rising of the dead as ghosts. Supposedly dead people's spirits returned to Earth at certain special times, in particular the annual celebration known as the "return of the dead,"

held in the month of Abu (July/August). Most ghosts naturally yearned to vent their anger and frustration by haunting the living during their brief excursion on Earth. But if they did give into this temptation, the sun god, Shamash, punished them (as if their repetitive and dull existence was not punishment enough). After the festival they had to return to the "Land of No Return."

With their conception of the afterlife so bleak, it is not surprising that most Mesopotamians were taught to make the best of their earthly lives. This is one reason why so many of them sought to be upright, honest, constructive citizens. Their motivation was not potential rewards that would come after death, but the desire not to waste the short time the gods had granted them on Earth.

Their grim view of the afterlife also explains the fascination the Sumerians and Babylonians had for the idea of attaining immortality. Their literature is full of stories of quests to find the secret of eternal life, most notably in the *Epic of Gilgamesh* and story of *Adapa*. Although the heroes of these tales search and search, they always fail in the end. The inevitable moral is that the gods will not share the gift of immortality with humans. In Gilgamesh's tale, the goddess Siduri tells the hero:

O Mighty King, remember now
that only gods stay in eternal watch.
Humans come, then go; that is the
way fate decreed on the Tablets

of Destiny. So someday you will depart, but till that distant day sing, and dance, eat your fill of warm cooked food and cool jugs of beer. Cherish the children your love gave life. Bathe away life's dirt in warm drawn waters. Pass the time in joy with your chosen wife. On the Tablets of Destiny it is decreed for you to enjoy short pleasures for your short days.[50]

In this and other ways, the religious beliefs of the ancient Mesopotamians shaped their views and lives in profound ways.

Chapter Seven

RELIGIOUS RITUALS AND FESTIVALS

The gods and the beliefs associated with them represented what might be called the conceptual part of religious worship in ancient Mesopotamia. In other words, these aspects of religion dealt with the basic concepts of who the gods were, how they had shaped the world, and what they expected of humans. The other primary part of worship was more practical or hands-on in nature. It consisted of the actual manner in which people communicated with and showed their admiration and respect for the gods. Included were erecting sacred temples; staffing these institutions with clergy (priests and/or priestesses); performing regular sacred rituals (including attempts to interpret the will of the gods); organizing and attending public festivals to honor the gods; and burying the dead in ways approved by both the gods and societal traditions.

Temples, Priests, and Priestesses

Temples always remained the central focus of community worship (although people also prayed and worshiped at home). Even before the Sumerians began building the first cities, agricultural villages usually featured a central structure dedicated to the gods and worship. These buildings were small and impermanent at first. But over time they became large, sturdy, and elaborately decorated. Nemet-Nejat explains that as the center of community worship and life, the temple also took on various commercial and social functions:

> The temple was regarded as the god's "house" or "estate," and managed like a secular institution. The temple could own property in more than one place and take part in various productive and commercial activities. The range

Mesopotamian Exorcisms

As shown most famously in the 1973 film, *The Exorcist,* exorcism is a process in which, supposedly, a demon or evil spirit is driven out of a person's body. Besides Christianity, several other religions have given credibility to exorcism, including the main belief system of ancient Mesopotamia. There, people thought that many kinds of illnesses were caused by demons or spirits inhabiting the body. And doctors known as *ashipu* specialized in spiritual cures, including exorcisms. Exactly how these rituals were performed is unknown. But they likely involved the recitation of special magical spells, washing and cleansing the body, and eating special diets. A surviving text describes the advice given to the Assyrian king Esarhaddon on how to get rid of a sickness-causing demon. The

king was to recite various spells, which followed strict formulas, or traditional wording; to avoid eating cooked foods; to wear a loose robe; and to go to the river to wash himself. Supposedly these acts would drive the demon away.

A bronze plaque from the ninth century B.C. depicts an exorcism of the demon Lamashtu. The demon god Pazuzu surveys a scene from above in which fish-clad priests attend to a sick person surrounded by animal-headed protective beings. Ultimately Pazuzu drives Lamashtu away.

of the temple's economic activities included cultivation of cereals, vegetables, and fruit trees; management of sheep, goats, and cows; manufacture of textiles, leather, and wooden

items; and promotion of trading links with foreign lands. . . . The temple also served as a forum for various judicial proceedings, particularly the taking of solemn oaths.[51]

As houses of worship, their main function, Mesopotamian temples differed from modern churches in an important way. Ordinary worshipers were not allowed to go inside the sanctuary (sacred enclosure or chambers) where the statues (called cult images) of the gods rested. On days set aside for communal worship, therefore, people crowded into open courtyards surrounding the sacred sanctuary.

The only people allowed to enter the sanctuary were clergy and the king (and perhaps members of his immediate family). A high priest was called an *en* and a high priestess an *entu*. Usually, high priests were men who performed the most sacred rites within the holy sanctuaries. Like regular priests, they had to meet strict requirements to enter the clergy. These included being literate, well educated, specially trained in religious matters, and free of physical deformities. High priestesses were less common and numerous than priests, but apparently no less respected. Held in particularly high esteem were the high priestesses of the moon god Nanna (or Sin) and love goddess Inanna (Ishtar). Priestesses were not allowed to have sex or children. (However, they *could* get married and act as stepmothers to any children their husbands already had.)

Mesopotamian priests and priestesses had diverse functions and duties. They handled divine statues and other sacred objects; performed purification rites (designed to ward off evil or impure spirits; interpreted signs thought to reveal the will of the gods; slaughtered animals in public sacrifices; advised kings on religious matters; and administered the temple estates. In matters relating to the gods themselves, the gender of the clergy assigned to a god was usually a crucial factor. With a few exceptions, males attended to male gods and females attended to goddesses.

Festival Day Celebrations

The most complex, sacred, and publicly visible duties of priests and priestesses were those performed during religious festivals. These took place at specially designated times of the year, like modern religious holidays do. The biggest and most eagerly anticipated festival was an agricultural celebration held at harvest time, most often in the month of Nisan, corresponding to today's March. (In a few places in Mesopotamia, the festival occurred twice, once at harvest time and again at planting time.) The Sumerians called it *Akiti;* the Akkadian (Babylonian and Assyrian) word for it was *Akitu*. Because the ancient Mesopotamian New Year came at harvest time, people often recognized it as a dual holiday and celebrated both simultaneously.

The exact length and details of the festival varied somewhat from era to era and place to place. Evidence shows that in Babylonia from the second millennium B.C. on, it lasted twelve days and involved a set series of rituals. These included prayer and the offering (sacrifice) of animals; formal processions in

The Uruk Vase, discovered in the Sumerian city of Uruk and dated to the fourth millennium B.C., depicts offerings to Innin, the goddess of fertility, during a New Year festival. Religious festivals containing special ceremonies and rituals to honor the gods were common throughout the centuries in ancient Mesopotamia.

which people marched, sang, and carried the divine cult images; reciting the *Epic of Creation* (which described the exploits of Babylonia's leading deity, Marduk); and both public and private feasts.

During the first six days of the festival, the local high priest conducted private ceremonies within the sacred sanctuary of the temple. The public, of course, was not allowed to witness these rituals. But the celebration's last six days featured lavish public rites. These honored not only Marduk, but also his divine son, Nabu, patron deity of scribes, literacy, and wisdom. A group of priests carried a statue of Marduk out of the temple and joined forces with the king and some of his nobles. There followed a solemn but festive procession witnessed by crowds of worshipers, well described by Georges Roux:

> [The parade] went down Procession Street, across Babylon in an aura of incense, songs, and music, while people were kneeling down in adoration as it passed by. Through Ishtar Gate, the [procession] left the city, and after a short journey on the Euphrates, reached [a] temple filled with plants and flowers in the middle of a large park.[52]

After three days of feasting and other activities, the worshipers returned to the city and bore the sacred image to Nabu's temple. There, at a blessed spot known as the "Shrine of Destinies," they hoped that either Marduk or Nabu would reveal whether or not the king and nation would enjoy success in the coming year. The high priest interpreted the divine message and announced it in dramatic fashion to the thousands of captivated worshipers.

After this high point of the festival, the worshipers feasted once more. Then the procession reversed its tracks and returned the image of Marduk to the main temple. At this point the king may have made love (in private) to a young woman specially chosen from the crowd of worshipers. If this ritual did indeed occur, it was probably intended to reenact the mythical marriage rites between the goddess Inanna and her companion, the divine shepherd Dumuzi.

In addition to universal religious festivals, like *Akitu,* which all Mesopotamians took part in, local peoples and regions had a number of rituals and celebrations of their own. One of these, for example, took place only in Babylon on the fifth day of the annual New Year's festival. Several priests thoroughly cleaned Nabu's shrine and then covered the cult image with a canopy made from cloth flecked with gold. The king entered the sanctuary and allowed the high priest to take off his crown and royal robes. Next, the priest slapped the king's face. The king then knelt before Nabu's image and swore that he had not abused the mighty authority the gods had granted him. This ceremony was designed to show that even kings were subject to the will of the gods.

Divining a God's Will

Not only during major festivals, but throughout the year, certain priests were expected to divine, or determine, the will of the gods, partly to ensure that the community did not suffer heaven's wrath. This process, which also included predicting future events, is called divination. Specially trained priests called *baru* carefully studied various natural phenomena, searching for divine signs. These included the livers or lungs of sacred animals; the behavior of animals, such as birds' flight patterns; the layout of cities; the movements of the heavenly bodies; the movements of clouds and puffs of smoke; and the rate of famines, floods, and disease epidemics. Any deviations from the "normal" patterns of these things were viewed as possible omens, divine signs of impending change, either good or bad.

When two such "abnormal" events occurred at the same time, the diviners were sure that they were dealing with a message from the gods. The belief was that this could not be mere coincidence. Instead one event must be associated with the other. For example, if a king died soon after an earthquake, the quake was seen as an omen foreshadowing the king's passing. As a result of these beliefs, Mesopotamian rulers almost always consulted their royal diviners before going on a journey or military campaign. If the signs were unfavorable, the trip or campaign might well be canceled.

It was thought that the will of the gods could also be determined via divine

The King and the Ravens

An example of ancient Mesopotamian divination appears in a surviving Assyrian text. King Esarhaddon asked his chief diviner to study and interpret the unusual behavior of some ravens he had witnessed. The diviner's answer was as follows:

As to Your Majesty's request addressed to me concerning the incident with the ravens, here are the relevant omens: "If a raven brings something into a person's house, this man will obtain something that does not belong to him. If a falcon or a raven drops something he is carrying upon a person's house or in front of a man, this house will have much traffic, [and] traffic means profit. If a bird carries meat, another bird, or anything else, and drops it upon a person's house, this man will obtain a large inheritance."

Quoted in Leo Oppenheim, ed., *Letters from Mesopotamia: Official, Business, and Private Letters on Clay Tablets from Two Millennia.* Chicago: University of Chicago Press, 1967, pp. 166–167.

messages sent through specially gifted people. These individuals were called oracles. (The messages themselves and the temples or other structures where the messages were conveyed were also referred to as oracles.) The Mesopotamians did not put as much faith in oracles as some other ancient peoples did. (The Greeks, for instance, strongly valued the famous Delphic Oracle, a priestess who dwelled in the temple of the god Apollo at Delphi, in central Greece.)

Still, the Sumerians, Babylonians, and some other Near Eastern peoples did consult oracles from time to time. There were two kinds. One was a prophecy made by an ordinary individual seen as being a medium between the gods and humans. Supposedly, a god might pay a visit to such a medium, or prophet (also sometimes called a frenzied person), either in a dream or when the person was awake. The other kind of oracle was, as in Greece, a member of the clergy. A priest or priestess might receive a divine message after directly questioning a god. The priest/oracle then relayed the message to the king. Such prophecies were often written down, as in the case of the following surviving example. An Assyrian priest delivered it to King Ashurbanipal (reigned ca. 668–627 B.C.), claiming it was the goddess Ishtar's promise to help the king defeat his enemies, the Elamites:

[When she spoke to me] the goddess Ishtar . . . was holding a bow in her hand, and a sharp word was drawn to do battle. You [the king] were standing in front of her and she spoke to you like a real mother. . . . She repeated her command to you as follows: "You shall stay here where you should be. Eat, drink wine, make merry, praise my divinity, while I go and accomplish that work to help you attain your heart's desire." . . . Then she went out in a frightening way to defeat your enemies, [namely the] king of Elam, with whom she was angry.[53]

It is important to note that kings did not always believe oracles and other forms of divination. Ashurbanipal's father, King Esarhaddon (ca. 680–669 B.C.), for example, executed a diviner whom he suspected of making up a supposed message from a god.

Burial Customs

No less important to a king than a divine message was being buried in an appropriate manner. And the same can be said of most of his subjects. They referred to death variously as "going to the road of one's forefathers," "going to one's fate," or "taking refuge on one's mountain." The belief was that one required proper preparation for this impending journey beyond Earth. This entailed washing the body of the deceased with oil and dressing him or her in clean clothes. It was also customary to sew the mouth shut. Then family members placed some personal items, such as combs or jewelry, beside the body.

Once the body was ready, the family held a wake. Relatives and friends came to mourn. Those families that

A coffin made of baked clay like this one, dating from the first century A.D. and adorned with decorations, was commonly used for burial in ancient Mesopotamia.

could afford it might hire professional mourners to make the gathering larger and thereby impress the neighbors. During the funeral procession, people sang sad songs and recited sad speeches and poems, not unlike the funeral speeches common today. The famous *Epic of Gil-* *gamesh* contains an example. The title character grieves the loss of his dearly departed friend, Enkidu, saying:

It is for my friend Enkidu that I weep. He brought joy to the feast. He was a shield before me in the

The excavation of a royal tomb at Ur reveals the skull of a woman who had been adorned with a gold headdress and a beaded necklace made of gold and lapis lazuli when she was buried in the late third millennium B.C.

The Power of Magic

In most ancient religions normal religious beliefs and rituals contained elements of what many people today would call magic. In Mesopotamia, for instance, people accepted that the gods had the power to wield magic, for both good and ill. In fact some gods, such as Enlil and Marduk, were thought to be skilled sorcerers. Magic took two main forms. One, black magic, involved the forces of evil, which people believed were always lurking nearby, ready to cause illness, accidents, bad fortune, or death. The other form of magic—white magic—supposedly had the power to counter the ill effects of black magic. White magic consisted of spells, incantations, burning figurines of demons, and other acts that were thought to drive evil away. Such rituals were most often performed by a diviner or spiritual doctor (*asipu*). To figure out what to do, he might consult a special text that contained lists of various illnesses and the traditional spells and cures for them. In contrast, practicing black magic was a crime. What's more, the law codes of ancient Mesopotamia provided laws to punish it.

confusion of battle. . . . Great evil has taken Enkidu my friend. . . . Enkidu your eyes no longer move. Why is that? . . . Enkidu I cannot feel the beat of your heart. Why is that? Great evil has taken Enkidu my friend. . . . May you Elders hear my words, I weep and I mourn for Enkidu [who] was my friend.[54]

Both during and after the funeral procession, it was customary for family members and close friends of the deceased to go unbathed and ungroomed. Some tore their clothes in an overt display of grief.

Most of the coffins carried and buried in these ceremonies were made of baked clay and were of modest cost. People who were very poor could not afford even these, so they wrapped the body in mats made of river reeds. The most common custom was to bury the coffin in the ground near the family house. That way the dead person's loved ones could feel near to him or her. Those who could afford it built a family crypt, usually directly beneath their home, and placed the coffin inside alongside those of other relatives who had passed on.

Not surprisingly, kings, queens, nobles, and rich people could afford much finer, more elaborate resting places. Archaeologists have found several royal Mesopotamian tombs, of which some of the most impressive were unearthed in the 1920s by Woolley at Ur. He excavated sixteen graves of kings and queens, who were buried with their servants. (These underlings likely drank overdoses of sleeping potion so that they could follow their masters and mistresses into the afterlife.) Most of these tombs had been looted in ancient times. But two were almost intact and included numerous grave goods such as jewelry, weapons, pottery, utensils, parlor games, and musical instruments.

These grave sites are, in a way, eerie and fascinating time capsules. Their contents, along with the remains of temples and surviving religious documents, are telling. They reveal a people long vanished who were as vital, moral, and devout in life and as mourned and missed in death, as anyone now living.

Notes

Introduction: The Past Is Present

1. Samuel N. Kramer, *Cradle of Civilization*. New York: Time-Life, 1978, p. 80.
2. Gwendolyn Leick, *The Babylonians*. London: Routledge, 2003, p. 129.
3. Rajiv Chandrasekaran, "A Gift from God Renews a Village." www.washingtonpost.com/ac2/wp-dyn/A10572-2003Oct10.
4. Stephen Bertman, *Handbook to Life in Ancient Mesopotamia*. New York: Facts On File, 2003, p. x.

Chapter One: Houses and Their Contents

5. Quoted in "The Code of Hammurabi." www.wsu.edu/~dee/MESO/CODE.HTM.
6. Gwendolyn Leick, *Mesopotamia: The Invention of the City*. New York: Penguin, 2001, p. 161.
7. Karen R. Nemet-Nejat, *Daily Life in Ancient Mesopotamia*. Peabody, MA: Hendrickson, 1998, pp. 123–124.
8. Quoted in "Mesopotamian Menus." www.saudiaramcoworld.com/issue/198802/mesopotamian.menus.htm.

9. Charles Leonard Woolley, *Ur of the Chaldees*. Ithaca: Cornell University Press, 1982, p. 50.
10. Nemet-Nejat, *Daily Life in Ancient Mesopotamia*, p. 154.
11. Xenophon, *Cyropaedia*. Trans. Walter Miller. New York: Macmillan, 1914, vol. 2, p. 325.

Chapter Two: Family, Women, and Children

12. Leick, *The Babylonians*, p. 73.
13. Steven J. Garfinkle, "The Assyrians: A New Look at an Ancient Power," in Mark W. Chavales, ed., *Current Issues and the Study of the Ancient Near East*. Claremont, CA: Regina, 2007, p. 57.
14. Leick, *Mesopotamia*, p. 117.
15. Leick, *Mesopotamia*, p. 179.
16. Quoted in "The Code of Hammurabi."
17. Quoted in "The Code of Hammurabi."
18. Quoted in "The Code of Hammurabi."
19. Quoted in "The Code of Hammurabi."
20. Bertman, *Handbook to Life in Ancient Mesopotamia*, pp. 284–85.
21. Trans. Nemet-Nejat, in *Daily Life in Ancient Mesopotamia*, p. 132.

Chapter Three: Life in the Community

22. Over time, as weather patterns changed, the gulf steadily receded southeastward; eventually, Ur lay in an arid region some 100 miles (161km) from the coast.
23. Nemet-Nejat, in *Daily Life in Ancient Mesopotamia,* p. 282.
24. Bertman, *Handbook to Life in Ancient Mesopotamia,* p. 257.
25. Daniel C. Snell, *Life in the Ancient Near East, 3100–332 B.C.* New Haven: Yale University Press, 1998, p. 106.
26. Gwendolyn Leick, *Historical Dictionary of Mesopotamia.* Lanham, MD: Scarecrow, 2003, p. 73.
27. Leviticus 24:19–21.

Chapter Four: Slaves and Serfs

28. Quoted in "The Code of Hammurabi."
29. Quoted in "The Code of Hammurabi."
30. Quoted in "The Code of Hammurabi."
31. Quoted in "The Code of Hammurabi."
32. Quoted in "The Code of Hammurabi."
33. H.W.F. Saggs, *Civilization Before Greece and Rome.* New Haven: Yale University Press, 1991, p. 56.
34. Quoted in "The Code of Hammurabi."
35. Quoted in "The Code of Hammurabi."
36. Saggs, *Civilization Before Greece and Rome,* p. 58.

Chapter Five: Games, Sports, and Travel

37. Norman B. Hunt, *Historical Atlas of Ancient Mesopotamia.* New York: Facts On File, 2004, p. 139.
38. Leick, *Mesopotamia,* p. 240.
39. Lionel Casson, *Travel in the Ancient World.* Baltimore: Johns Hopkins University Press, 1994, pp. 23–24.
40. Casson, *Travel in the Ancient World,* pp. 25–26.
41. Quoted in "Sumerian Praise Poems." www.realhistoryww.com/world_history/ancient/Misc/Sumer/Praise_poems2.htm.

Chapter Six: Gods and Religious Beliefs

42. Samuel N. Kramer, *History Begins at Sumer.* Philadelphia: University of Pennsylvania Press, 1981, p. 101.
43. Bertman, *Handbook to Life in Ancient Mesopotamia,* p. 115.
44. Quoted in Kramer, *Cradle of Civilization,* p. 102.
45. Georges Roux, *Ancient Iraq.* New York: Penguin, 1993, p. 92.
46. A.T. Olmstead, *History of the Persian Empire.* Chicago: University of Chicago Press, 1966, p. 98.
47. Chester G. Starr, *A History of the Ancient World.* New York: Oxford University Press, 1991, p. 280.
48. Leick, *The Babylonians,* p. 155.
49. Kramer, *Cradle of Civilization,* p. 106.
50. Quoted in "The Tablets Telling the Epic of Gilgamesh, Tablet 10."

www.mythome.org/gilgamesh10.
html.

Chapter Seven: Religious Rituals and Festivals

51. Nemet-Nejat, in *Daily Life in Ancient Mesopotamia,* p. 188.

52. Roux, *Ancient Iraq,* p. 400.
53. Quoted in James B. Pritchard, *The Ancient Near East, Vol. 2.* Princeton: Princeton University Press, 1976, pp. 170–71.
54. Quoted in "The Tablets Telling the Epic of Gilgamesh, Tablet 8." www. mythome.org/gilgamesh8.html.

Glossary

abum: The word for "father" in ancient Akkadian (the language spoken by the Babylonians and Assyrians).

amulet: An object thought to have magical and protective powers.

animism: A belief system that holds that spirits inhabit rocks, trees, rivers, and other aspects of nature.

baru: In ancient Mesopotamia, specially trained priests who examined the organs of animals to determine the will of the gods.

birthing stool: A low, wooden stool with an open space in the seat. A pregnant woman sits on the stool and her baby descends through the open space.

bronze: An alloy, or mixture, of the metals copper and tin.

cesspool: A hole in the ground into which pipes carrying human waste flow.

cistern: A basin or other shallow container used to capture rainwater.

cult image: A statue of a god, usually resting inside a temple.

cylinder seal: A small, curved piece of stone (or other material) on which people etched images or words.

daevas: In the ancient Persian religion, wicked followers of the evil being Ahriman.

debt slavery: In many parts of the ancient world, the temporary enslavement of a person or persons to pay off a debt they owe.

diorite: A hard black stone, often used for jewelry, figurines, and marker stones.

en: A Sumerian priest; a priestess was an *entu*.

felt: Crushed sheep's hair.

harmamaxa: A large carriage with a roof and curtains on the side to provide privacy for the passengers.

hostel: An inn or other lodging for travelers.

karum: In ancient Mesopotamia, a guildlike organization of merchants.

lapis lazuli: A semiprecious stone with a bluish hue.

martum: The word for "daughter" in ancient Akkadian.

marum: The word for "son" in ancient Akkadian.

me (*parsu* in Akkadian): Divine rules guiding nature and human affairs.

monogomous: Having only one wife (or husband).

naditu: Very religiously devout and often celibate Babylonian women who lived in secluded, nunnery-like structures.

nard: An early form of backgammon played in ancient Persia.

pantheon: A group of gods worshiped by a people or nation.

patriarchal: Male dominated.

patrileneal: A system of inheritance in which land and other property pass from father to son.

procession: A parade, often religious in nature.

qanat: An Arabic word denoting an aqueduct in Mesopotamia.

relief (or bas-relief): A carved scene raised somewhat from a flat surface.

scribe: In the ancient world, a person who used his or her reading and writing skills in some professional capacity.

secular: Nonreligious.

serf (or *villein*): An agricultural worker who, though not a slave, was dependent on the landowner financially and otherwise.

shatrang: An early form of chess played in ancient Persia.

stele (or stela): An upright stone or metal slab or marker bearing images, words, or both.

unleavened bread: A flat bread made without yeasts (which make bread rise).

ummum: The word for "mother" in ancient Akkadian.

wardum: Slaves in ancient Babylonia.

Time Line

B.C.
ca. 3300–3000
The Sumerians begin building the world's first cities in southern Mesopotamia.

ca. 3000
Bronze begins to be used in large quantities in Mesopotamia.

ca. 2300
The first known empire, centered in north-central Mesopotamia, is established by Akkadian ruler Sargon the Great.

ca. 2275
The Akkadian ruler Rimush takes four thousand captives and enslaves them.

ca. 2094–2047
Reign of the Sumerian king Shulgi, who builds several hostels to accommodate travelers.

ca. 1792–1750
Reign of the Babylonian king Hammurabi, who issues a famous law code.

ca. 1760
Hammurabi captures the kingdom of Mari, on the upper Euphrates.

ca. 1700
The chef of the king of Mari writes a cookbook that survives to the present.

ca. 1400
Assyrian men and women begin wearing wide robes belted at the waist.

ca. 1200
Iron smelting begins in Mesopotamia.

ca. 1115–1077
Reign of the Assyrian king Tiglath-pileser I, who becomes known for his large-scale hunting expeditions.

ca. 722–705
Reign of Sargon II, who builds the first underground aqueducts in the region.

ca. 700
Mesopotamia begins importing cotton from Egypt.

ca. 559
Cyrus II becomes Persia's first king and soon afterward begins building an empire.

ca. 522–486
Reign of Persia's third king, Darius I, who issues coins called *darics* for both financial and political purposes.

334
The Macedonian Greek king Alexander the Great begins his swift conquest of the Persian Empire.

A.D.
634–651
Muslim Arab armies conquer much of Sassanian-controlled Mesopotamia and other parts of the Near East.

For More Information

Books

Enrico Ascalone, *Mesopotamia: Assyrians, Sumerians, Babylonians*. Berkeley: University of California Press, 2007. This book gives a well-written and nicely illustrated overview of the major peoples of early Mesopotamia.

Stephen Bertman, *Handbook to Life in Ancient Mesopotamia*. New York: Facts On File, 2003. This is a fact-filled, easy-to-read guide to the region's peoples, leaders, religious beliefs and myths, social customs, languages, arts and crafts, and much more.

Jean Bottero, *Everyday Life in Ancient Mesopotamia*. Baltimore: Johns Hopkins University Press, 2001. A noted scholar examines living conditions in the ancient Mesopotamian empires.

John Farndon, *Mesopotamia*. London: Dorling Kindersley, 2007. This is a beautifully illustrated survey of ancient Mesopotamian history, culture, and life, accessible to readers of all ages.

Norman B. Hunt, *Historical Atlas of Ancient Mesopotamia*. New York: Facts On File, 2004. This book contains several sections on ancient Mesopotamian culture, life, and beliefs.

Samuel N. Kramer, *The Sumerians: Their History, Culture and Character*. Chicago: University of Chicago Press, 1971. A valuable source of information about early Mesopotamia, this book also contains much about everyday life and beliefs.

Gwendolyn Leick, *Mesopotamia: The Invention of the City*. New York: Penguin, 2001. This book gives a detailed examination of life in key Mesopotamian cities, including housing, royal hunts, worship, and much more.

Karen R. Nemet-Nejat, *Daily Life in Ancient Mesopotamia*. Peabody, MA: Hendrickson, 1998. This is one of the more comprehensive sources on the subject presently available.

Susan Pollock, *Ancient Mesopotamia*. New York: Cambridge University Press, 1999. Readers will enjoy this well-written survey of ancient Mesopotamian history and culture.

Michael Roaf, *Cultural Atlas of Mesopotamia and the Ancient Near East*. New York: Facts On File, 1990. This well-illustrated book provides a useful overview of the lives and world of the ancient Mesopotamian peoples.

Daniel C. Snell, *Life in the Ancient Near East, 3100–332 B.C.* New Haven: Yale University Press, 1998. This book offers a sweeping overview of ancient Near Eastern culture, customs, and ideas.

Web Sites

Achaemenid Royal Inscriptions (www.livius.org/aa-ac/achaemenians/inscriptions.html). This Web site contains translations of several ancient Persian inscriptions.

Ancient Mesopotamia: Archaeology (http://oi.uchicago.edu/OI/MUS/ED/TRC/MESO/archaeology.html). This site, run by the famed Oriental Institute of the University of Chicago, features several links to brief but excellent articles about ancient Mesopotamia.

The Code of Hammurabi (www.wsu.edu/~dee/MESO/CODE.HTM). On this site visitors will find a good translation of the famous Babylonian ruler's laws.

Persia (http://ragz-international.com/persians.htm). This site offers a brief but informative overview of Persian history, with numerous links to related topics.

The Sumerians (http://home.cfl.rr.com/crossland/AncientCivilizations/Middle_East_Civilizations/Sumerians/sumerians.html). Here visitors will find a good general overview of the Sumerians for younger readers, including a useful map of early Mesopotamia and several color photos.

The Tablets Telling the Epic of Gilgamesh (www.mythome.org/Gilgamesh.html). This is the home page for an excellent translation of Gilgamesh's epic tale, with which all ancient Mesopotamians were familiar.

Index

Wars, 13
Water supplies, 41–43
Weights and measures, 36–37
Wheels, 64
Wine, 21
Women
    clothing styles for, 21, 23
    in family structure, 26
    high-status, 26–28
    inheritance by, 29, 31
    makeup worn by, 23–24
    status and duties of, 28–29
Wool, 21–22

Woolley, Charles Leonard, 8, 21–22, 86
Wrestling, 60, 62–63
Writing, invention of, 14

X
Xenophon, 24

Z
Zoroaster, 72–73
Zoroastrianism, 72–73

Picture Credits

Cover photo: © 2008/Jupiterimages
Ali Al-Saadi/AFP/Getty Images, 12
The Art Archive/Archaeological
   Museum Aleppo Syria/Gianni Dagli
   Orti, 71, 74
The Art Archive/Bibliothèque des Arts
   Décoratifs Paris/Gianni Dagli Orti,
   22
The Art Archive/British Museum/
   Alfredo Dagli Orti, 59
The Art Archive/Gianni Dagli Orti, 15
The Art Archive/Musée du Louvre
   Paris/Gianni Dagli Orti, 63
Bildarchiv Preussischer Kulturbesitz/
   Art Resource, NY, 80

© British Museum/Art Resource, NY,
   39, 61
Werner Forman/Art Resource, NY, 23
© Werner Forman/Corbis, 46
David Furst/AFP/Getty Images, 10
Gale, Cengage Learning, 9
Erich Lessing/Art Resource, NY, 18, 21,
   26, 27, 30, 32, 38, 41, 48, 51, 54, 57,
   62, 69, 78, 83
John D. McHugh/AFP/Getty Images,
   11
© Kazuyoshi Nomachi/Corbis, 72
Réunion des Musées Nationaux/Art
   Resource, NY, 43
Scala/Art Resource, NY, 84

About the Author

Historian and award-winning writer Don Nardo has published many books about the ancient world, including *Life in Ancient Athens, The Etruscans, Life of a Roman Gladiator, Religion in Ancient Egypt,* literary companions to the works of Homer, Sophocles, and Euripides, histories of the Assyrian and Persian empires, and Greenhaven Press's encyclopedias of ancient Greece, ancient Rome, and Greek and Roman mythology. He lives with his wife, Christine, in Massachusetts.